Eating Disorders

OTHER BOOKS OF RELATED INTEREST

Eating Disorders

Shasta Gaughen, *Book Editor*

Daniel Leone, *President*
Bonnie Szumski, *Publisher*
Scott Barbour, *Managing Editor*
Brenda Stalcup, *Series Editor*

Contemporary Issues
Companion

GREENHAVEN
PRESS®

THOMSON
™
GALE

San Diego • Detroit • New York • San Francisco • Cleveland
New Haven, Conn. • Waterville, Maine • London • Munich

LIBRARY OF CONGRESS CATALOGING-IN-PUBLICATION DATA

Eating disorders / Shasta Gaughen, book editor.
    p. cm. — (Contemporary issues companion)
  Includes bibliographical references and index.
  ISBN 0-7377-1620-7 (pbk. : alk. paper) — ISBN 0-7377-1619-3 (lib. : alk. paper)
    1. Eating disorders. I. Gaughen, Shasta. II. Series.
  RC552.E18E282113 2004
  616.85'26—dc21
                                                                    2003055107

Printed in the United States of America

OCT   2007

CONELY BRANCH

CONTENTS

Chapter 4: Overcoming Eating Disorders

FOREWORD

In the news, on the streets, and in neighborhoods, individuals are confronted with a variety of social problems. Such problems may affect people directly: A young woman may struggle with depression, suspect a friend of having bulimia, or watch a loved one battle cancer. And even the issues that do not directly affect her private life—such as religious cults, domestic violence, or legalized gambling—still impact the larger society in which she lives. Discovering and analyzing the complexities of issues that encompass communal and societal realms as well as the world of personal experience is a valuable educational goal in the modern world.

Effectively addressing social problems requires familiarity with a constantly changing stream of data. Becoming well informed about today's controversies is an intricate process that often involves reading myriad primary and secondary sources, analyzing political debates, weighing various experts' opinions—even listening to first-hand accounts of those directly affected by the issue. For students and general observers, this can be a daunting task because of the sheer volume of information available in books, periodicals, on the evening news, and on the Internet. Researching the consequences of legalized gambling, for example, might entail sifting through congressional testimony on gambling's societal effects, examining private studies on Indian gaming, perusing numerous websites devoted to Internet betting, and reading essays written by lottery winners as well as interviews with recovering compulsive gamblers. Obtaining valuable information can be time-consuming—since it often requires researchers to pore over numerous documents and commentaries before discovering a source relevant to their particular investigation.

Greenhaven's Contemporary Issues Companion series seeks to assist this process of research by providing readers with useful and pertinent information about today's complex issues. Each volume in this anthology series focuses on a topic of current interest, presenting informative and thought-provoking selections written from a wide variety of viewpoints. The readings selected by the editors include such diverse sources as personal accounts and case studies, pertinent factual and statistical articles, and relevant commentaries and overviews. This diversity of sources and views, found in every Contemporary Issues Companion, offers readers a broad perspective in one convenient volume.

In addition, each title in the Contemporary Issues Companion series is designed especially for young adults. The selections included in every volume are chosen for their accessibility and are expertly edited in consideration of both the reading and comprehension levels of the audience. The structure of the anthologies also enhances accessibility. An introductory essay places each issue in context and provides helpful facts such as historical background or current statistics and legislation that pertain to the topic. The chapters that follow organize the material and focus on specific aspects of the book's topic. Every essay is introduced by a brief summary of its main points and biographical information about the author. These summaries aid in comprehension and can also serve to direct readers to material of immediate interest and need. Finally, a comprehensive index allows readers to efficiently scan and locate content.

The Contemporary Issues Companion series is an ideal launching point for research on a particular topic. Each anthology in the series is composed of readings taken from an extensive gamut of resources, including periodicals, newspapers, books, government documents, the publications of private and public organizations, and Internet websites. In these volumes, readers will find factual support suitable for use in reports, debates, speeches, and research papers. The anthologies also facilitate further research, featuring a book and periodical bibliography and a list of organizations to contact for additional information.

A perfect resource for both students and the general reader, Greenhaven's Contemporary Issues Companion series is sure to be a valued source of current, readable information on social problems that interest young adults. It is the editors' hope that readers will find the Contemporary Issues Companion series useful as a starting point to formulate their own opinions about and answers to the complex issues of the present day.

INTRODUCTION

Bright, attractive young women between the ages of twelve and twenty-five. Hardworking, conscientious, and eager to please. Driven to achieve perfection—even if they have to starve themselves to reach it. These personality characteristics are typically found among individuals who have eating disorders, the most common of which are anorexia nervosa, bulimia nervosa, and binge-eating disorder. Experts estimate that one out of every hundred young women has anorexia, while bulimia affects as many as 3 to 4 percent of college-aged women. According to recent studies, approximately 1 percent of women suffer from binge-eating disorder, while an astonishing 30 percent of women who seek help to lose weight exhibit behaviors associated with binge-eating disorder.

Eating disorders can have serious physical consequences. Without appropriate medical treatment, up to 20 percent of sufferers will die. Even among those who do receive treatment, approximately 3 percent die from complications of their disorder, and many others develop severe health repercussions. Full recovery is difficult to attain; even with medical and psychological treatment, 20 percent of patients achieve only a partial recovery, marked by periodic setbacks and relapses. Sadly, another 20 percent do not even partially recover but, despite professional help, remain locked in the disorder's grip.

Of the three main eating disorders, anorexia is the most dangerous physically and has the lowest recovery rate. Anorexia is characterized by an extreme fear of becoming overweight and by an obsession with dieting and thinness. The disorder involves drastic weight loss, at least 15 percent below what would be considered a normal and healthy body weight. However, people with anorexia usually perceive themselves as being fat and will strenuously fight attempts to get them to eat. They may also exhibit bizarre, compulsive behaviors such as dividing their food into perfectly equal portions, lingering for hours over tiny meals, or obsessively categorizing foods into groups that are "good" or "bad." Often they become depressed and withdraw from their friends and family.

Most researchers believe that individuals of a certain personality type are at greater risk for developing anorexia. The typical anorexic is a perfectionist, an overachiever, a people pleaser who craves approval and strives to avoid conflict. At the same time, however, anorexics feel insecure and inadequate. They tend to be afraid of change and do not adapt well to new situations. According to Anorexia Nervosa and Related Eating Disorders (ANRED), an organization that is part of the National Eating Disorders Association, people with anorexia often "fear growing up, taking on adult responsibilities, and meeting the demands of independence." As a result, they try to assert their independence and demonstrate control over their lives by strictly regulating their weight and their food intake. This obsession with thinness serves as a symbolic way for anorexics to express deep, powerful emotions that they find difficult to face.

As they continue to starve themselves, anorexics may develop serious health problems, including the cessation of menstrual periods, a decrease in muscle mass and bone density, and cardiac distress. Nevertheless, anorexics "insist they feel fine, or they minimize their discomforts and continue to work hard, get good grades in school, perform athletically, or exercise compulsively," states physician Diane W. Mickley, founder of the Wilkins Center for Eating Disorders in Greenwich, Connecticut. If their weight drops to life-threatening levels, anorexics may be hospitalized, and even then they may go to the extreme of tearing out feeding tubes or secretly exercising to burn off what little food they have been forced to eat. While recovery from anorexia is possible, the success rates are very low: A recent study found that only 33 percent of anorexics fully recover from the disorder.

Bulimia, also known as binge-purge disorder, is similar to anorexia in that it involves an unhealthy fixation with food and weight. However, instead of self-starvation, the disorder is characterized by cycles of bingeing and purging. Bulimics consume abnormally large quantities of food in a short period of time and then try to rid their bodies of the excess calories through the use of laxatives, self-induced vomiting, rigorous exercise, or some combination of the three. In many cases, people with bulimia do not become dangerously thin, and therefore they can usually conceal their eating disorder better than anorexics can. Yet bulimia can also be life threatening, since repeated vomiting or overuse of laxatives can result in malnutrition, severe dehydration, gastric ruptures, kidney failure, or cardiac arrest.

Like anorexics, individuals with bulimia are usually depressed and withdrawn, even though they may put up a cheerful front. Despite appearances to the contrary, ANRED explains, bulimics "have problems trusting other people. They have few or no truly satisfying friendships or romantic relationships." In addition, bulimics often have difficulties with impulse control; a high percentage not only binge on food but also exhibit other impulsive behaviors, such as sexual promiscuity, shoplifting, or alcohol and substance abuse. According to eating disorders expert Sheila M. Reindl, "a person with bulimia nervosa typically fears she is hollow, bad, even rotten at her core and works hard to avoid experiencing a core sense of shame." Because of their sense of guilt about their behavior, people who have bulimia strive to keep their eating disorder secret, while at the same time attempting to project an image of independence and competence to the world.

Anorexia and bulimia have long been recognized as diagnosable medical conditions; binge-eating disorder, on the other hand, was not formally categorized until 1992. In marked contrast to anorexics and bulimics, people who suffer from binge-eating disorder are likely to be overweight or obese. This disorder is typically characterized by periodic binges (as with bulimia, but without the subsequent purging) or continuous overeating. People who have binge-eating disorder go on diets repeatedly, but they almost always fail to permanently lose weight. In fact, dieting may contribute to the problem by causing these individuals to crave food more than ever until they break their diet with a massive binge episode. During a binge, people with this disorder often experience a fugue state in which they become mentally and emotionally detached from their actions. Researchers have suggested that the binges may serve as a way to numb emotional pain.

Eating disorders are commonly associated with young women, who are far more likely to suffer from the problem than any other segment of the population. However, experts estimate that approximately 10 percent of all people with eating disorders are male. In their book *The Adonis Complex: The Secret Crisis of Male Body Obsession*, physicians Harrison G. Pope Jr. and Katharine A. Phillips and clinical psychologist Roberto Olivardia note that until recently, much of the research focused on women because conventional wisdom held that eating disorders rarely occurred among men. Now, "that wisdom is changing," they write. "We're seeing more and more eating disorders of all types in men . . . probably in response to changing societal standards of male body image." Even more alarming, individuals of both genders are developing eating disorders earlier than ever—some children have been diagnosed as young as six. Furthermore, while eating disorders were once thought to only affect people from affluent nations like the United States, they are now beginning to show up in less developed parts of the world.

The dramatic rise in the incidence of eating disorders in recent years makes it even more crucial for society to address this disturbing problem. The essays included in *Eating Disorders: Contemporary Issues Companion* serve as a starting point for readers to learn more about the different types of eating disorders that increasingly affect people of all ages, genders, races, and cultures. This informative volume provides an overview of the nature of eating disorders, considers the possible causes of these disorders, and presents the moving personal stories of those who suffer from disordered eating. In the final chapter, authors discuss various approaches to treatment and offer hope that—despite the difficulties of recovery—eating disorders can in fact be overcome.

CHAPTER 1

EATING DISORDERS: AN OVERVIEW

The Facts About Eating Disorders

Marcia Herrin and Nancy Matsumoto

In the following excerpt from their book *The Parent's Guide to Childhood Eating Disorders*, Marcia Herrin and Nancy Matsumoto cover three major eating disorders—anorexia nervosa, bulimia nervosa, and binge-eating disorder. They describe the warning signs and symptoms of each disorder, explain the physical and behavioral problems that people with eating disorders typically face, and offer reasons for what may trigger disordered eating. Furthermore, the authors note that patients often exhibit symptoms of more than one eating disorder at a time. Herrin is the founder and codirector of the Dartmouth College Eating Disorders Prevention, Education, and Treatment Program. She also has a private practice specializing in the treatment of eating disorders. Matsumoto is a writer who contributes to such publications as *Time*, *Newsweek*, the *New York Times*, and the *Los Angeles Times*.

Ruth, age thirteen, is well adjusted, at the top of her class academically, and loves to play soccer. Her mother, Susan, has been somewhat worried about Ruth's recent weight loss, but reassures herself that Ruth looks nothing like the images of girls suffering from eating disorders that she has seen on television talk shows and in magazines. Instead of ghoulishly skeletal, Ruth really looks cute, athletic, slim, and energetic. One day, however, while straightening up Ruth's room, Susan comes across a diary in an open drawer. She can't resist taking a peek, thinking that it might shed light on Ruth's recent weight loss. Susan learns that Ruth has thrown up for the first time the night before. Although she has been trying to self-induce vomiting for a number of weeks up until now, this is her first success. Ruth writes that she is relieved that vomiting is not very hard to do once you figure it out, and that she is confident she can continue doing it. Susan replays recent changes in Ruth's behavior—occasional dizziness, the significant reduction in her food intake, the way she was eager to bake a birthday cake for her brother but refused to eat any of it herself. She realizes that she has been oblivious to the early signs of an eating disorder in her daughter, a disorder which, left untreated, could become life threatening.

Most people know what the extreme emaciation of full-blown anorexia looks like, and some of us might even be able to recognize some of the telltale signs of chronic bulimia, the swollen cheeks, or trips to the bathroom after every meal. But recognizing an eating disorder before it reaches these stages is trickier. In this selection, we will describe the different types of eating disorders.

Although we separate anorexia, bulimia, and binge-eating disorder into neat categories, often people will go from being an anorexic to a bulimic, or the reverse, or even exhibit all the hallmarks of both disorders at the same time. . . .

Anorexia Nervosa

The anorexic child refuses to maintain even a minimally normal body weight. She is intensely afraid of gaining weight, a fear that is fueled by a distorted perception of her body's shape and size. No matter how thin she gets, she sees herself as fat and unattractive, and this distortion in perception usually becomes more severe the more weight she loses. Some anorexics who have not yet reached adulthood will not necessarily lose weight. Instead, they may fall short of expected weight gains while still increasing in height. Others will not grow at all and may be permanently stunted in height unless they begin to eat better.

Anorexic girls who have already begun menstruating stop getting their periods due to their starving bodies' abnormally low levels of estrogen. Among girls who have not yet reached puberty, menstruation may be delayed or completely inhibited by anorexia. In all of these cases, lack of estrogen poses serious risks to bone health of girls. Boys' bones can also be affected by starvation-induced hormonal changes. In anorexic boys, lowered levels of testosterone can lead to reduced bone density.

The History of Anorexia

Self-imposed starvation is an ancient disorder that dates back to medieval times. In the Europe of the thirteenth century, historical records tell of women saints who fasted and refused food as part of their religious practice. In 1689, one of the earliest cases of what is now known as anorexia involved a sixteen-year-old English boy.

By the 1870s the term *anorexia nervosa*, meaning loss of appetite due to emotional reasons, had been coined to describe the self-starvation found primarily among upper-middle-class western European and American girls. The historian Joan Jacobs Brumberg, author of the book *Fasting Girls*, argues that modern anorexia is distinct from early cases because of its body-image concerns triggered by "mass cultural preoccupation with dieting and a slim female body."

There are two subtypes of anorexics. The first is the restricting type. The anorexic of this subtype loses weight simply by reducing her food intake, fasting, or engaging in excessive and lengthy periods of exercise as a means of working off calories. The second subtype is the binge-eating/purging type. She restricts her intake as well, but alternates this behavior with bouts of binge eating and often purging. The purging can take the form of self-induced vomiting or the abuse of laxatives, diuretics, or enemas. Some anorexics of this type don't binge, but still purge after consuming even small amounts of food.

Often anorexia nervosa is triggered by a stressful life event—leaving home for the first time to enter boarding school, summer camp, or college, being teased about one's weight, breaking up with a boyfriend, not getting chosen for a sports team, or problems within the family, such as divorce. Other risk factors include affluent and well-educated parents, early feeding problems, low self-esteem, high neuroticism (overly moody, sensitive, or fearful), an overprotective mother, having a relative with anorexia or bulimia, especially a parent or sibling (identical twins are particularly at risk in that if one develops an eating disorder, the other is at high risk), and childhood sexual abuse. . . .

Common Traits and Beliefs of the Anorexic

The child who is becoming anorexic often becomes obsessive about counting calories and fat grams and begins to exclude foods she perceives as fattening. Sometimes she will turn to vegetarianism, ostensibly to "eat more healthily," but in fact as a way of controlling her intake of high-fat foods. Often the anorexic exhibits an increased interest in food labels and extreme concern, even fear, of eating fat. Other anorexics, however, especially younger anorexics, simply restrict food intake, seemingly with little interest or awareness about how many calories or fat grams those foods contain. It is not uncommon for the anorexic to eventually eat only a limited number of foods and approach those foods in a ritualistic, programmed way. She may cut up her food into small pieces, or chew each bite of food a certain number of times, or she may constantly sip diet sodas or other no-calorie drinks to fill her stomach.

The anorexic does not always believe that she is overweight. She may acknowledge that she is thin, but wants to be even thinner, and is still bothered by certain aspects of her body that she insists are too big. Prime areas of dissatisfaction are the abdomen, buttocks, and thighs. The anorexic often weighs herself obsessively, constantly assesses her figure in the mirror, or makes up other ingenious ways of measuring fat. A patient of mine was convinced she was too fat unless she could see prominent veins on her arms. Another of my patients was only satisfied when a coin fit in the hollow of her collarbone. The regular taking of thigh or waist measurements with a tape measure is another commonly used method, along with lying down to assess how sunken the anorexic's stomach is compared to her hipbones. Patients have told me that they do this by putting a ruler across their abdomen and making sure that the stomach and the ruler do not touch.

As the above examples illustrate, anorexics often have obsessive personalities, are perfectionistic and driven to achieve. Although they may be highly intelligent and accomplished, their self-esteem gradually comes to be largely based on the shape and weight of their body. Weight loss becomes a sign of self-discipline, a huge achievement. Conversely, they view weight gain as a sign of failure, the result of a pitiable lack of self-control. Although anorexics often perceive themselves to be very well educated in matters of nutrition and exercise, they may in fact harbor many misconceptions about these topics. Those that are aware of the serious medical consequences of anorexia often find it hard to believe that their own case is dire enough to result in such problems. When they finally do realize it is, the patterns of self-starvation are often too entrenched, and the anorexic tries to hide his or her disorder and deny any medical problems. . . .

Mood and Behavioral Problems

The secondary problems that result from self-starvation include depression, social withdrawal, irritability, and insomnia.

Obsessive-compulsive behavior is common, leading the anorexic to think constantly of food, even to develop an interest in cooking, collect recipes, and hoard food but not eat it. Teenagers with eating disorders who have jobs often find themselves working in food-related establishments. One reason, of course, is that these are the positions most readily available to teenagers. Yet it also seems that eating disorders often propel affected teenagers toward these jobs.

Bethany told me that while working in the local ice-cream shop she would slip into the walk-in ice-cream freezer to surreptitiously eat ice cream, even though her extreme thinness made the cold almost unbearable, and even though she would never allow herself to do such a thing in the presence of others. As Bethany's story illustrates, the mind of the starving adolescent naturally focuses on food, almost to the exclusion of everything else.

While anorexics often have obsessive or perfectionistic personalities *before* the onset of their disorder, and indeed are at higher risk to become anorexic because of those traits, this is not always the case. Researchers believe that obsessive-compulsive behaviors like Bethany's can also be caused or magnified by the effects of starvation on the body and are not necessarily characteristics of the anorexic herself. . . .

The anorexic may dislike eating in public, suffer from feelings of ineffectiveness, and be inflexible and controlling of her environment. She also often has difficulty expressing herself emotionally. The anorexic of the binge-eating/purging subtype is more apt to have difficulty controlling her impulses, therefore is more likely to abuse alcohol or other drugs, engage in activities such as shoplifting, and exhibit more mood swings.

There is some evidence that the secondary mental disturbances among those whose anorexia does develop before puberty are more serious. In younger anorexics, who are less likely to have been affected by peer or cultural pressure to diet, it is more likely that the eating disorder is an indication of underlying emotional problems (overly perfectionistic nature, low self-esteem, or obsessive-compulsive traits, for example), rather than the emotional problems being a by-product of the eating disorder.

Yet in most cases, after the eating disorder is resolved, these children regain their emotional equilibrium. They have learned to better manage these emotional issues and are more resilient for having endured the disorder. As painful, dangerous, and difficult as these disorders can be, many of my patients have described overcoming an eating disorder as a character-building experience.

How Prevalent Is Anorexia?

There has been a remarkable increase in anorexia among teenagers in recent years, making it the third most common chronic condition among adolescent girls after obesity and asthma. Among adults, the prevalence of anorexia has remained constant in recent years, with possibly as high as 4 percent of American girls and women suffering from anorexia at some time during their lives.

Anorexia among children, although less well documented, appears to be increasing as well. Parents should also be aware that contrary to popular belief, boys are not immune to anorexia. Although only one-tenth of the adult population of anorexics are men, among adolescents, boys account for up to one-third of all anorexics. . . .

The Course of Anorexia

The course of anorexia among different patients is extremely variable, especially if no treatment is provided. Some anorexics recover after a brief episode, some will experience alternating bouts of weight gain and then relapse, and others' condition will steadily decline over many years. Others may move quickly into life-threatening anorexia with little forewarning. Some will go on to develop bulimia or binge-eating disorder. Having anorexia increases a person's risk of dying by more than twelve times the expected rate, with deaths most often resulting from starvation, suicide, or severely low potassium levels. Because anorexia is such a dangerous and potentially life-threatening disorder, early detection and prevention is critical. Research, in fact, has shown that early, aggressive treatment protects against mortality. Effective treatments for eating disorders are now available, yet because anorexics will often deny their illness or attempt to conceal it, it is not uncommon for there to be significant and costly delays between the onset of the disorder and the beginning of treatment.

Bulimia Nervosa

Instead of the self-starvation that is characteristic of anorexics, bulimics engage in periodic bouts of binge eating. These are always followed by a period of contrition during which the bulimic tries to undo the effects of the binge, either by purging, abusing diuretics or laxatives, or fasting and/or exercising to the extreme.

Although there are scattered references to bulimia-like behavior from the ancient Greeks onward (the Roman vomitorium was the designated site for forced vomiting between banquet courses), bulimia is a modern and quite recent phenomenon. The word *bulimia* is derived from a Greek word that can be literally translated as "ox hunger." The word has been used medically for hundreds of years to describe excessive, ravenous hunger. Descriptions resembling what we know as bulimia today—bingeing followed by purging—began to emerge in the 1930s. The incidence of this behavior increased after World War II, and by the 1960s bulimia was described as a feature of some anorexic patients. An epidemic-sized increase in the 1970s among college-aged women led to the recognition of bulimia as a distinct eating disorder. In 1979 the term *bulimia nervosa* was officially coined to describe an eating disorder that is related to anorexia, with the added clinical features of bingeing and purging.

There are two subtypes of bulimia, the purging type and the non-purging type. In the first, the bulimic regularly engages in self-induced vomiting or the abuse of laxatives or diuretics after a binge. The non-purging subtype refers to someone who binges, but compensates by fasting or excessive exercise instead of vomiting or taking laxatives or diuretics.

The triggers to a binge can vary from depressed mood to the extreme hunger that results from stringent dieting or feelings of self-loathing related to the bulimic's own weight or shape. Often the onset of bulimia is preceded by a stressful or traumatic event, such as leaving home for the first time, being criticized for being fat, a death or illness in the family, breaking up with a boyfriend, starting high school, starting to menstruate, suffering a disfiguring accident, a first sexual experience, or an abortion.

Having siblings or a parent who suffers from bulimia, depression, or alcoholism increases a child's risk of becoming bulimic, most likely because of a potent combination of both genetic and environmental triggers.

Common Traits and Beliefs of the Bulimic

Like the anorexic, the bulimic's self-esteem is based to an excessive degree on her own body shape and weight. Like the anorexic, the bulimic tries to restrict food intake, but eventually fails, usually by engaging in a binge. (We should note that such a "failure" is perfectly normal behavior after a period of self-starvation, although the bulimic does not see this.) A period of often severe restriction follows, usually ending in another binge. Binges are defined as eating far more than most people would eat during a discrete period of time. Binges can begin in one place and continue in another; for example, at a party at a restaurant, and then in the privacy of the bulimic's bedroom or bathroom. Different people binge on different sorts of food, but the binge usually includes sugary, high-calorie foods.

Unlike the anorexic, who may be proud of her ability to restrict her intake of food, the bulimic is usually mortified by and ashamed of her own behavior. She tries to hide her problem, and is often highly effective at doing so. She may steal food to binge on in secret, use her allowance money to buy binge food, or make sure to run the shower when throwing up so no one hears her.

Once a binge begins, the bulimic eats rapidly, almost without thinking, until she feels discomfort or even outright pain from her excessive consumption.

While anorexics revel in the feeling of total control over their own eating, bulimics during a binge feel a total lack of control. Their binges, especially during the early stages of the disorder, may put them into a state of frenzy, or even beyond that, trigger a sense of dissociation, the feeling of not even inhabiting the body that is doing such damage to itself. The binge is usually followed by a crash in mood, and the return of depressive or self-loathing feelings.

Bulimia can sometimes be harder for parents to detect because the typical bulimic is within normal weight range and because of the secretive nature of the eating and purging behaviors. Some research has indicated that before the onset of the disorder, the child (this is especially true of boys) is more likely to be overweight than his or her peers.

Purging Behaviors, Fasting, and Exercise

Purging, or vomiting to compensate for a binge, is used by 80 to 90 percent of the bulimics who are treated in eating-disorder clinics. Purging offers immediate relief from the often acute feelings of discomfort that follow a binge, and the sense of "undoing" the caloric damage the bulimic has done to his or her body. It is after purging that bulimics once again feel in control and a sense of well-being returns. They feel light, their stomach is flat once again, and they feel they have fixed, or erased, their problem. Purging is usually followed by a period of dieting: restricting calories and avoiding fattening foods or foods the bulimic fears may trigger another binge. Purging may also be followed almost immediately by another binge, then another purge and so on. Most younger patients do not have enough unsupervised time to develop such a destructive pattern of behavior, but for those who do, this cycle can go on for hours. My college-age patients tell me their binge-purge cycles can last for a whole day or evening.

Bulimics induce vomiting most often by using their fingers or other instruments such as a spoon or toothbrush to stimulate the gag reflex. They may use laxatives and diuretics as another way of purging, and in rare cases even resort to enemas or, to induce vomiting, syrup of ipecac.

Bulimics may also compensate for their binges by fasting for a day or even longer, or exercising to excess. Exercise is considered excessive when it significantly cuts into important activities, when the child engages in it at odd times or in odd settings (getting up in the middle of the night to run in place, or on car trips, running around the car at rest stops), or when the child pursues a taxing regimen despite an injury or other medical complication. . . .

Problems Associated with Bulimia

Bulimics are more apt to suffer from depressive symptoms or anxiety disorders than the average person, but it seems that often the onset of the mood and anxiety disturbance coincides with the development of the disorder. Once the bulimia is effectively treated, these disturbances disappear. Adolescent bulimics are also more prone to substance abuse problems, which occur in about a third of all sufferers. Bulimics will often begin stimulant use, caffeine, nicotine, NoDoz, as a means of controlling their appetite. They may abuse diet pills or prescription medications belonging to friends or parents.

The physical health of most bulimics, unless they are underweight, is not as compromised as that of anorexics. Yet they tend to be more aware of and concerned about their physical symptoms, and they report more physical complaints than anorexics. They will often report nonspecific symptoms such as "heartburn" or feeling "bloated," without giving all the information necessary to make the diagnosis of bulimia. In some cases they don't link their symptoms to their bulimia. In others, they are torn between wanting to hide the disorder and wanting to be confronted about it by a physician or parent. Embarrassed by or ashamed of their problem, they throw out clues that fall short of a confession.

Kellie, a chronic bulimic, would spontaneously vomit when leaning over. Unaware that this is a very common occurrence with chronic bulimia, she was sure she had a serious intestinal disease. Kellie convinced her mother, who had suspected Kellie was struggling with bulimia but wasn't sure, to make an appointment with a gastroenterologist. Kellie's mom hoped the doctor would get to the bottom of the problem. As is often the case in such situations, however, Kellie's mom did not inform the doctor of her suspicions. Kellie accurately described her symptoms, but because she failed to mention her history of bulimia, she ended up with medicines and advice for a symptom that was caused by her bulimia, while the bulimia itself remained untreated.

How Prevalent Is Bulimia?

The prevalence of bulimia among adolescent and young adult women is estimated to be as high as 5 percent of the population. The prevalence of bulimia in males has yet to be established, but researchers report that of all bulimic patients, 10 to 15 percent are male.

Unlike anorexia, which we suspect is on the increase among children, bulimia appears to be quite rare in younger children. Practitioners are, however, seeing younger and younger teenagers with bulimia. Until now, it was thought that bulimia usually strikes slightly older adolescents than does anorexia, commonly making its appearance from mid-adolescence through the college years. That may be changing as bulimia becomes more prevalent among quite young adolescents.

In my own practice, a number of my college-age patients tell me that they have been bulimic since sixth or seventh grade. One reason researchers may be overlooking bulimic children is that most bulimics wait a number of years before seeking treatment or before their illness is discovered.

The Course of Bulimia. The binge eating of bulimia often begins during or after an episode of dieting. This restricted eating may lead to some weight loss, after which bingeing and purging begin to predominate. The course of bulimia ranges from chronic to intermittent bouts interspersed with periods of remission.

Binge-Eating Disorder

Children and adolescents suffering from binge-eating disorder engage in periodic episodes of binge eating, but do not regularly follow it up with any of the compensatory measures described in the previous section on bulimia.

Binge eaters suffer the same inability to control their food intake as bulimics. They eat rapidly during a binge, almost without thinking, even when they are not hungry. They usually binge secretly, ashamed of and repulsed by their own behavior. Yet hard as they try, they are unable to stop bingeing. When a binge is over, they feel a combination of disgust at their behavior, guilt, and often depression. Most often, bingeing occurs as a consequence of repeated and unsuccessful efforts to diet.

Binge eating may be detected when there is evidence of eating in secret, lying about eating, or food disappearing, although some children without an eating disorder will engage in such behaviors if parents are overly restrictive in allowing them access to food. Being overly restrictive in turn increases the child's risk of developing an eating disorder.

Like bulimics, binge eaters suffer a great deal of distress over their inability to stop eating once they have started a binge. But the binge eater does not induce vomiting, does not misuse laxatives or diuretics, does not regularly fast or exercise excessively the way the bulimic does. Binge eaters may occasionally engage in some of these behaviors, but not regularly, as bulimics do.

The History of Binge Eating

Albert Stunkard, one of the premier researchers in binge eating, pointed out that binge eating is the oldest of all the eating disorders, one that has deep historical roots and may go back more than two millennia. Binge eating was described by early writers like Homer and Hippocrates and is discussed in early medical literature. It was not until the mid-eighteenth centry, however, that binge eating was described as a pathology. By the turn of the nineteenth century, it was firmly established as an aberrant behavior.

When binge eating was first described in the modern medical literature in 1959 it was almost immediately classed as an occasional practice of anorexics. Later, when bulimia was identified, binge eating came to be considered characteristic of bulimia. Only since the mid-1990s has binge-eating disorder been recognized as a separate and unique eating disorder. Even now, however, more research must be done before binge-eating disorder becomes an official eating disorder diagnosis.

Common Triggers

Binge eating may be triggered by depression and anxiety, feelings that often are put at bay or relieved by a binge. The binge eater may turn to food as a comfort in the face of a family disturbance, or trouble at school.

Often a child or adolescent begins bingeing after losing a significant amount of weight from dieting. Much research, in fact, has been done showing that habitual dieting leads to binge eating. Dieters attempt to restrict their food intake, only to overcompensate by bingeing. One study done on former World War II prisoners of war found that the veterans, who suffered dramatic weight loss while in captivity, reported significantly higher frequency of binge eating than those veterans who had not been imprisoned and starved. Largely based on studies such as these, the current medical opinion on binge eating is that often it is the body's natural response to starvation—or the modern-day equivalent, the weight-loss diet.

Elyse had always been on the "chunky" side, but was determined to enter high school at a lower weight. To do so, she had to reduce her intake of calories to less than 300 calories per day. Even then, she was unable to lose as much weight as she wanted. Eventually she found herself binge eating between bouts of dieting. Over time this pattern of diet-binge-diet caused her weight to creep up to even higher than it was when she started dieting.

Characteristics of the Binge Eater

The onset of the disorder typically occurs in late adolescence or the early twenties, although in my practice I have seen an increasing number of younger adolescents and even children who are binge eating. Binge eaters tend to be more overweight than other eating-disordered patients and experience more dramatic fluctuations in weight. Binge-eating disorder does not necessarily lead to weight gain, however, particularly among adolescents with active metabolisms, or among young athletes. Parents can miss a serious problem of binge eating because their child is normal weight. Although the binge eating of the normal-weight child may not seem to be anything to worry about, vigilance is advised because binge eating can lead to other eating disorders. A common scenario is the binge eater who over time gains weight, which in turn triggers bulimia or anorexia. Binge eating can also lead to low self-esteem since most people who binge eat feel very guilty and ashamed about this behavior.

David, a fourteen-year-old patient of mine, tells me he feels physically addicted to binge eating. He desperately wants to stop, but finds that he cannot.

Binge eaters like David report that their disorder interferes with their relationships with other people and their ability to feel good about themselves, as well as higher rates of self-loathing, disgust about body size, depression, and anxiety about weight gain. Like bulimics, those who suffer from binge-eating disorder are more prone to substance abuse than the general population.

Latryce, who began bingeing after unsuccessfully trying a severely restrictive diet, eventually resorted to taking an herbal supplement containing ephedrine. An amphetamine stimulant that has been associated with cardiac problems, ephedrine has led to a number of deaths. Despite her therapist's warnings about the dangers of the supplement, Latryce found that she was unable to make herself stop taking it.

How Prevalent Is Binge Eating?

Binge eating differs from anorexia and bulimia in that the incidence among females and males is closer to parity. Approximately 40 percent of binge-eating disorder cases occur in boys and men.

Among children, although there are no published scientific studies to back this up, my clinical experience has led me to believe that there is a clear increase in the number of those suffering from binge-eating disorder in recent years.

I have also noticed that although I treat about an equal number of girls and boys for binge eating in my practice, parents tend to be more concerned when a daughter binge-eats than a son. Because it is more socially acceptable for boys to have a big appetite than for girls, a serious binge-eating problem in a boy may be overlooked.

Brad, a young patient of mine, had to gain 50 pounds before his binge eating was recognized as a problem by his parents and pediatrician. Gina's parents, on the other hand, were quick to consult me after hearing that one of Gina's close friends dieted and binged at the summer camp both girls attended. They worried that Gina, a lovely, shapely fourteen-year-old, might be at risk. They knew she struggled with the fact she wasn't as thin as she wanted to be and they wanted advice on how to be proactive.

The tremendous rise in obesity among young people in our country has been well documented, but has been largely ascribed to lack of exercise, increase in junk food consumption, and super-sized American servings. The severely overweight kids that I see in my practice are also binge eating, which I believe is another reason for the significant increase in obesity among American children.

Eating Disorders Not Otherwise Specified

Because so many people who are treated by eating disorders programs do not fit neatly into the category of anorexics or bulimics, the American Psychiatric Association has established another category, eating disorders not otherwise specified (EDNOS). EDNOS is the designation that professionals use for eating disorders that do not meet all the criteria for anorexia or bulimia and is considered a distinct class of eating disorder in and of itself.

People who fall into this category may, for example, exhibit all of the characteristics of anorexia including severe weight loss, but still have menstrual periods, or they may still manage to maintain a weight in the normal range in spite of radically reduced food intake. The latter happens most often with larger or obese children; no one suspects they have anorexia because even severe weight loss does not leave them visibly malnourished. In other cases of EDNOS, patients may binge by chewing and then spitting out rather than swallowing most of their food.

EDNOS is particularly common among adolescents with eating disorders, whose disorders might not be as dire or entrenched as those of older patients. Bulimia is diagnosed as EDNOS when it has occurred for less than three months or when binge-purge episodes occur less than twice a week.

I tell parents not to assume that just because their child is diagnosed as having EDNOS that the child's problem is insignificant and does not need treatment. They can be in as much physical danger as the classic anorexic or bulimic, and suffer just as much emotional distress.

Although we have described three types of eating disorders as separate phenomena, in real life they are not always that clear-cut. An anorexic, as we have described, may alternate self-starvation with periods of bingeing, and even purging. It is quite common for a restricting-type anorexic, after engaging in months or years of fasting and superhuman self-restraint, to finally give in to her incessant thoughts and cravings about food and become a binge eater or a bulimic. In fact, up to 50 percent of patients with anorexia develop bulimic symptoms, and some people who start out as bulimics develop the symptoms of anorexia.

BEYOND DIETING: THE DRIVE TO BE THIN

Karen Goldberg Goff

Experts estimate that one in a hundred adolescent girls suffers from an eating disorder, according to Karen Goldberg Goff, a staff writer for the *Washington Times*. Because teenage girls are frequently on diets, she relates, it is often difficult to discern when a teenager has moved beyond dieting to an eating disorder. However, the author reports, there are specific signs—such as depression, isolation, a marked increase in physical activity, avoidance of certain foods, and ritualized eating behaviors—parents can watch for that may indicate that their child has developed an eating disorder. While research shows that eating disorders may have genetic components, she writes, the media's emphasis on the desirability of being thin may also be a contributing factor. Parents should avoid focusing on thinness or dieting and instead model healthy eating habits for their children, Goff recommends.

There was rapid weight loss and a diet that temporarily consisted only of oranges. There was a large amount of time spent in the bathroom and avoiding food or bingeing on it.

These were the first clues Stephanie Watt had that her then-12-year-old daughter, Kristen, had an eating disorder.

Mrs. Watt and her husband, Mike, got Kristen the help she needed to deal with anorexia and bulimia. Kristen, a normally outgoing soccer player and top student, lost 50 pounds in less than five months and over the next two years went through two inpatient counseling programs.

Even after returning to a normal weight, however, Kristen's body had been through too much. Her electrolytes were dangerously out of balance. She died suddenly in July 1999.

"Every day I blame myself," Mrs. Watt says. The Stockton, Calif., woman has started a foundation in her daughter's name to raise awareness of eating disorders and help parents and health professionals understand the signs, symptoms, causes and treatment.

"There were signs I continually missed," she says. "Even in the hospital, we never thought she was in a high-risk situation. You never think you can die."

Kristen Watt's situation was extreme, but she was among an estimated one in 100 adolescent girls suffering from anorexia (intense fear of getting fat and refusal to eat) or bulimia (binge eating followed by vomiting or laxative abuse), says Dr. Angela Guarda, a psychiatrist and director of the Eating Disorders Clinic at Johns Hopkins University Hospital.

"It is very common for parents, in retrospect, to say they didn't notice at first," Dr. Guarda says. "They didn't put the puzzle together. One reason is because about 60 percent of teen-age girls are dieting."

The difference between dieting and having an eating disorder can be tough to gauge, Dr. Guarda says. When dieting becomes an obsession, it is time for parents to step in, she says.

"The difference between a normal dieter and one with an eating disorder is that dieting has become a ruling passion in the latter," Dr. Guarda says. "Individuals often describe being preoccupied with food and weight 90 percent of the time."

Other early clues are restrictive eating behaviors. A person with an eating disorder will start eliminating entire groups of food, such as those that contain fat, and narrowing food choices, Dr. Guarda says. Most of the teens she counsels say they are vegetarians. That proclamation should be a red flag for parents, she says.

"This can be a key sign to notice," she says. "Ask them what kind of a vegetarian they are. Are they eating Indian curry that is loaded with ghee (butter)? Or just salad? A lot of the world is vegetarian, but they also eat fat. In a person with an eating disorder, fat is the component of food they typically limit."

An exaggerated increase in exercise should pique a parent's interest, too. While some daily physical activity is healthful, an anorexic or bulimic person often will become obsessive about working out, the psychiatrist says.

"She may become agitated if she can't work out," Dr. Guarda says. "If the family is going on an outing, the daughter panics because she can't go on her morning run."

A patient with an eating disorder will show signs of depression and social isolation, Dr. Guarda says. Because many social situations have to do with food, an anorexic will avoid those situations.

Another situation an anorexic will avoid is family mealtime, she says.

"She may develop food rituals such as eating slowly, refusing to eat with the family or refusing to eat food prepared by others," Dr. Guarda says. "It is not uncommon for me to see patients who have not eaten with their parents for a year. Sometimes this goes unnoticed since family meals are not the norm anymore. It makes it hard for parents to pick it up. Sometimes the first time they notice is at Thanksgiving."

Eventually, people with an eating disorder also become obsessed with food. Extreme hunger gives way to reading labels and cookbooks and eventually in about 50 percent of cases, binge eating.

"Within six months to a year of severely limiting their food intake, many anorexics will begin to binge-eat the foods they have not allowed themselves to eat," Dr. Guarda says. "Signs of this include bags of cookies disappearing, candy wrappers in the room and weight gain."

Bulimia is a much harder eating disorder to catch because many bulimics are a normal weight, says Dr. Tomas Silber, a specialist in adolescent medicine at Children's National Medical Center.

"Many times when parents find out, it is just a matter of luck," Dr. Silber says. "They catch their child throwing up in the bathroom."

A less apparent sign of repeated vomiting is swollen salivary glands, says Dr. Silber. Swollen salivary glands will give a bulimic a "chipmunk cheek" appearance, he says. Some bulimics have scabs on their knuckles from putting their hands in their mouths to induce vomiting, he adds. Others have teeth that are severely damaged by stomach acid.

Kristen Watt followed a typical pattern from anorexia to bulimia. Mrs. Watt, like many parents, found out about Kristen's vomiting by looking in the bathroom and at her daughter's clothes.

"She wasn't real good about covering her tracks," Mrs. Watt says. "She spent large amounts of time in the bathroom. I would find clothing with vomit on it."

Who Gets an Eating Disorder?

Kristen's condition began around the same time as puberty, a typical time for young girls to develop disordered eating, Dr. Silber says.

"Boys and girls are similar until puberty," he says. "Then a remarkable difference takes place. When secondary sex characteristics start to occur, boys acquire muscle mass and girls acquire fat mass. This is normal, but it goes to a girl's thighs and buttocks as preparation for eventual childbearing. Many young girls are not prepared for this, and they misinterpret this as getting fat rather than getting female."

Ten times more girls than boys have eating disorders, but some boys also develop anorexia or bulimia, Dr. Silber says.

"Traditionally, we see it in boys who have to make weight, such as in wrestling," he says. "Or sometimes a boy might be pudgy and he gets teased, so he becomes fanatical."

Though eating disorders can happen in any family, both Drs. Guarda and Silber say there is a typical patient profile.

"I would say a high-risk patient is one who belongs to the upper middle class or upper class," Dr. Silber says. "She belongs to a family who is concerned about the body and appearances. She may have low self-esteem but be a high achiever in many areas. A genetic history of alcohol, depression or eating disorders adds tons of risk."

Two studies last year showed that scientists are gaining a better understanding of the role of genetics and eating disorders.

Researchers at the University of Pittsburgh compared rates of eating disorders among 1,831 family members of 504 women ages 18 to 28 with anorexia or bulimia.

Dr. Michael Strober, lead author of the study, says nearly 12 percent of women with severe anorexia had female relatives who had some symptoms of the disease. Four percent of the women with bulimia also had relatives with bulimia.

"The rate of bulimia and anorexia nervosa among female relatives of persons with eating disorders was between four and 11 times higher compared with incidents of illness in women without relatives with an eating disorder," Dr. Strober says.

At Virginia Commonwealth University [VCU] in Richmond, doctors studied rates of anorexia and depression among 2,163 female twins, both fraternal and identical. Overall, 77 women (3.6 percent) had been diagnosed as suffering from anorexia, and six of the women had a twin who shared the diagnosis.

Though researchers admit that is not a huge percentage, it is enough for them to say that genes influence a susceptibility to the disorder.

They also found that 140 sets of twins suffered from major depression, leading researchers to believe there is a genetic component to both disorders. Past research has indicated that 50 percent of women with anorexia have major lifetime depression.

The VCU study authors said living in a shared environment may be somewhat responsible for twins' propensity toward an eating disorder.

Dr. Guarda says it is not likely one single gene is responsible for eating disorders. The cause more likely is a combination of a genetic propensity combined with environment, she says.

"The media has taken a lot of flak" for promoting a thin, ideal woman, she says, "but not everyone is getting an eating disorder. Only 3 percent of the population develops clinical anorexia or bulimia. The media's focus on thinness may be lowering the threshold and increasing rates of eating disorders, but it is not the whole answer."

What Parents Can Control

The focus on thinness does not stop at adulthood. In many families, girls begin asking if they look fat or going on diets because they are emulating their mothers, says Abigail H. Natenshon, a Chicago psychotherapist and author of the book "When Your Child Has an Eating Disorder: A Step-by-step Workbook for Parents and Other Caregivers."

"Parents need to be role models in what they say and do," Ms.

Natenshon says. "Parents need to be an emotionally healthy role model and a role model for healthy eating. One of the reasons eating disorders are so prevalent is that we have forgotten what healthy eating is."

Dr. Silber agrees.

"I tell mothers to stop talking about dieting," he says. "It is the same as with parents who are smokers. Just because they smoke, it does not give their teens license to smoke."

Another way to instill healthful eating habits is to sit down to meals as a family as much as possible, Ms. Natenshon says.

"Making meals and sitting down together is the best way to observe a child's behavior," she says. "Too many kids are fending for themselves because we are too busy to eat together. They are eating fast food and Power Bars. Kids tell me they believe dieting is the only way to keep their weight down."

At those family meals, talking will go a long way, Ms. Natenshon says. Start a dialogue about dieting, she advises.

"Ask your child, 'What are your dieting goals? How did you decide this is the best way to lose weight?'" Ms. Natenshon says. "Many parents don't take eating disorders seriously until it is too late. This is one of the most lethal mental health disorders, but if detected and treated early enough, it is curable in a majority of cases.

"Parents owe it to their children to educate themselves and take eating disorders seriously," she says. "They have to know that eating disorders are not going to show up in the doctor's office—kids will keep it a secret—or in lab tests. It is going to show up at home, in the bathroom and at the kitchen table."

THE RISE OF EATING DISORDERS AMONG PRETEEN GIRLS

Laura Meade Kirk

Eating disorders usually strike young women in their teens or twenties. However, as Laura Meade Kirk points out in the following selection, girls are increasingly beginning to develop eating disorders at a younger age. Experts have found that many young girls are evidencing concern about dieting and body image as early as first grade, Kirk reports. As girls approach puberty, the author explains, they may attempt to fight their natural weight gain through excessive dieting and exercise, which can lead to disordered eating habits. She notes that preteen girls with eating disorders face greater medical risks than do older patients: Because they are still growing, any sudden weight loss can quickly and significantly harm their health. Kirk is a staff writer for the *Providence Journal Bulletin* in Rhode Island.

At first, she simply wanted to wear a tankini.

She was 11 and a little on the chunky side—not fat, but with enough of a belly that her mom suggested that she looked better in a one-piece bathing suit. But she was tired of boxy T-shirts and baggy pants. She'd just started middle school and she wanted to wear tight-fitting shirts and low-cut jeans like her friends.

Mostly, she wanted that tankini—a two-piece bathing suit with a tank-top style top and hip-hugging bottoms.

So, in early 2002, she told her mom she was giving up sweets. No more Oreos and Chips-Ahoy after dinner, a staple at her house. No more Little Debbie fudge-like brownies. No more Skittles.

Over the next five months, she dropped a few pounds and sprouted several inches. She was 5-foot-2 and 108 pounds. She celebrated her 12th birthday in the spring of 2002 by buying a bright flowered tankini. Everyone said she looked great.

That's when the trouble began, she recalled. "I figured, 'Why not lose some more weight and look even better?'"

She basically starved herself the rest of the summer until, in the fall of 2002, she was hospitalized. Her heart muscle was so weak it could have stopped at any time.

This girl, who asked to be called Allison, was among nearly 20 kids ages 8 to 12 admitted to Hasbro Children's Hospital in Providence, Rhode Island, during 2002 with life-threatening conditions caused by eating disorders. And those are just the ones who got sick enough to wind up in the hospital.

Disturbing Statistics

The numbers underscore a disturbing trend: Kids are developing eating disorders at increasingly younger ages.

The National Eating Disorders Association (NEDA), in Seattle, can provide no clear statistics on the number of girls under age 12 who suffer from eating disorders. "There still tends to be a lot of secretiveness, and not everyone seeks help," notes Holly Hoff, a project director for the association.

But NEDA surveys have found:

- 51 percent of all girls ages 9 and 10 say they feel better about themselves if they're on a diet.
- 46 percent of all 9- to 11-year-old girls say they are "sometimes or very often" on diets.
- 82 percent of these girls say that their families are "sometimes or very often" on diets.

That, Hoff said, "highlights the very critical role that parents play" as role models for their kids about weight. "When mom talks about not wanting to wear a bathing suit, or just being on the latest crash diet, kids pick up on that."

She said these messages are going out to even the youngest children. Surveys show that 42 percent of girls in grades 1 to 3 say they want to be thinner.

Hoff, who uses puppet shows to teach young children the dangers of dieting, said, "What's amazing to me is hearing first graders ask me, 'What is better, Slim Fast or Weight Watchers?'"

She said, "I had one darling tiny little girl who raised her hand and said, 'I don't want to wear blue jeans because they make my ankles look too fat.'"

Traditionally, Hoff said, teens have been most at risk for developing eating disorders—especially during "times of major physical and emotional life changes," such as puberty and heading off to college.

But today, girls are going through puberty at a much younger age, says Jennifer Aspel, a Providence, Rhode Island, psychologist who specializes in the treatment of eating disorders. And typical teenage concerns about body image and dieting are also affecting these much younger girls.

Add the influence of pop culture that promotes the wafer-thin body look, the media barrage about dieting and weight issues, and an increase in societal pressures for kids of all ages, Aspel said.

No wonder she's now seeing middle and elementary school kids with significant eating disorders—at younger ages than ever before.

These children face even greater medical risks than older girls with similar disorders, said Dr. Suzanne Riggs, director of adolescent medicine at Rhode Island Hospital and Hasbro Children's Hospital, who heads the team of specialists that treats these kids when their dieting becomes deadly. Because they're still growing, even a small weight loss can quickly and dramatically affect their health.

It strips their bodies of good fat as well as bad, affecting everything from menstruation and bone density to the brain's ability to function, Riggs said. They lose so much muscle that even their hearts are at risk.

Consider Allison's case: Most 12-year-olds have a normal resting heart rate of at least 60 beats per minute. Allison's was barely 50 when her mom brought her to Hasbro Children's Hospital for a checkup in the fall of 2002.

Riggs immediately admitted Allison to the hospital's intensive care unit. Riggs told Allison's mom: "If we let her go home, her heart could stop tonight."

Her mom burst into tears.

"I couldn't believe what they were telling me," her mom recalled. "How could it have gotten this bad, this fast? . . . I was just sobbing—sobbing and shaking. I couldn't believe this was happening."

An Unhealthy Obsession

Allison's mom had been worrying for months about her daughter's diet. First, her daughter had given up sweets. Then fat. She refused peanut butter sandwiches. She ate salads without dressing. She'd pick at dry toast or sandwiches with a single slice of turkey—no mayo. She swapped cereal for Carnation Instant Breakfast, and she toyed with dinner with her family. Soon, she barely ate anything.

Allison had also become obsessed with exercise, her mom said. Right after dinner, she'd race outside to the trampoline and start jumping furiously. Or, she'd suddenly drop to the floor and grind out 50 or 60 sit-ups.

"At first," her mom said, "I thought [her diet] was great. I thought, 'It's good you want to be healthy.'"

But then she watched her daughter shrink, dropping from a misses' size 5 pant to a girls' 14—a size she hadn't worn in more than three years.

Her mom tried to force her to eat, but worried about pushing too far. "Do I make her eat, or do I not make her eat? What's the best thing to do? I don't know. And no one could tell me."

It all came to a head when Allison traveled to Florida with her grandmother in August 2002, and she began shivering uncontrollably in the 80-degree heat. Her mom knew something was desperately wrong. She met her daughter at the airport and called her pediatrician on her cell phone during the drive home.

Allison was mad. "There's nothing wrong with me. I'm fine!" she insisted.

But the pediatrician figured Allison now weighed about 95 pounds, and he agreed it was time to see a specialist. He gave Allison's mom the names and numbers of a variety of specialists in Boston and Providence.

She felt clueless. "What did I know about eating disorders? I'm feeling totally isolated, abandoned, and I didn't know where to turn."

Finally, she learned of Dr. Riggs and her program at Rhode Island Hospital. It took five weeks to get an appointment.

Her mom recalls: "I cried every night for five weeks."

The Classic Signs

Allison was experiencing what experts say are the classic signs of an eating disorder:

She had a sudden, drastic change in her diet. She was obsessed with weight and body image. She insisted on checking food labels for fat grams and calories, and refused to eat entire categories of food. She exercised excessively. She was losing fat and muscle as well as energy. She couldn't concentrate in school.

She says her friends in her public middle school didn't say much about her weight loss. Most of them thought she was just naturally skinny.

But in some schools, weight loss becomes a competition of sorts—especially among certain groups of girls who tend to be ambitious, overachievers who aim to please adults, Riggs said.

This attitude can be fueled by some mothers—and fathers—who focus too much on body image—theirs or their daughter's, Riggs says.

These moms are constantly dieting, and going to the gym, and even having cosmetic surgery. Often they encourage their daughters to do the same.

Some schools can also inadvertently foster eating disorders, Riggs said. She recalls one all-girls school that assigns parts for the annual school show based on body size. They have some costumes for thin girls and some for heavy girls, so they essentially hand out parts based on a child's weight.

At another all-girls school, the so-called "anorexics table" in the lunchroom is where the girls who don't want to eat lunch sit during the lunch period, one parent said.

But the problem isn't confined to girls schools, Riggs was quick to add. It's also found in co-ed schools, and it crosses socio-economic and racial borders.

Some coaches foster eating disorders by encouraging athletes, especially those in competitive sports and dance classes, to diet to "make weight" or "look good" for the judges, Riggs said.

In fact, she said, an increasing number of boys are suffering from eating disorders—either because of sports or parental and peer pressure to have flat abdomens and look good in tight-fitting pants.

Growing Kids Need to Gain Weight

All this is just plain wrong, says Riggs and other experts.

"It's tough to change the cultural mindset," says Steve Emmett, founder and executive director of the Anorexia and Bulimia Association of Rhode Island. "We need to teach people it's what's inside that counts."

Kids—and their parents—need to accept that they're going to put on weight as they approach puberty.

Some girls will put on 20 to 50 pounds in a year, says Hoff, of the National Eating Disorders Association. Some kids fill out before adding inches in height. Others gain inches, then fill out. But they need to know that their bodies will even out over time.

Riggs thinks no child should be encouraged to lose weight—especially not those who are approaching or entering puberty. They need that weight to grow the way their bodies are meant to grow.

And some kids have to face genetic facts: They're born with certain body types, and that's out of their control.

"Some kids are predispositioned to be one weight or another," said Dr. David Herzog, a professor at Harvard School of Medicine and president of the Harvard Eating Disorders Center at Massachusetts General Hospital. "Their bodies are built differently."

"All kids go through rough spots, heavy/slim," Riggs said. But ultimately, "what weight and shape you have is not a personal choice."

So parents and others have to preach, and practice, healthy lifestyles—from healthy diets to staying active—as role models for their kids, Aspel said.

"We need to find better ways of identifying beauty or attractiveness in ourselves," Herzog said. "Weight is one, but humor, optimism, athleticism, all contribute to our attractiveness as people." And we need to emphasize that to our kids, he said.

If a child is losing weight, parents should contact a doctor, Riggs said. Not all weight loss is caused by eating disorders. Some are a result of other medical problems. But in general, she and others said, the only time a child should be placed on a weight-loss diet is when a pediatrician—not weight-conscious parents—decide that it's a medical concern.

"It's when the behaviors become extreme, when the preoccupation [with weight] becomes extreme, that's when we begin to get concerned," Aspel said.

Even then, pediatricians need to be more attuned to how they address weight issues—and the risks weight loss can pose, Riggs and others said.

She cited the case of one young man, recently admitted to the hospital after his weight dropped from 210 pounds to 110 in 8 months and his heart rate was a meager 19 beats per minute. She called the boy's doctor, who said he'd been monitoring the boy's weight loss. The doctor said the boy's heart rate had been "in the 30s" for the past several weeks and perhaps months.

Riggs shook her head at the thought. This boy could have died.

And he was under a doctor's care.

Parents Should Take Charge

Some, such as Emmett, say more needs to be done to make society more accepting of the fact that people come in all sizes and shapes so kids don't feel the pressure to look like a supermodel.

Parents also need to talk to their kids about weight issues and take the focus off losing weight as a way to look good.

Beauty is more than skin deep.

"When kids 9, 10, 11 years old are talking about [how] they hate themselves, they hate their bodies, they're too fat. . . . It should be taken seriously," Aspel said. "There should be some discussion. At the same time, a parent's initial instinct is, 'If my child's unhappy with how they're looking, let's change it.'"

But consider non-diet approaches, she suggested. Look at ways the entire family can change their diets and physical habits.

Indeed, Riggs said, parents need to take control of meals. It's their job to choose the foods, prepare the meals and insist the kids eat. The bottom line, she said, is "food is the medicine and you have to eat it all."

Others compare food to the fuel needed for a car to run. Kids need to understand the importance of this.

And schools need to do more to educate children, as young as kindergartners, about the perils of diets and eating disorders, Riggs said. But they've resisted, often because they don't have the time or money to expend on the curriculum.

So some parents groups have stepped up to bat.

Brenda Abramovich, chairwoman of the Parent Action Committee of seven independent schools in Rhode Island, has been busy compiling a program on eating disorders that will be hosted by the Lincoln School in Providence and is open to the public.

One of the students at Lincoln's elementary school was recently hospitalized for severe medical complications stemming from an eating disorder, and many of the parents there are understandably concerned, Abramovich said. "They're equally surprised and frightened it could happen this young."

But the issue affects a variety of students and families, not just at

Lincoln, which is why she wanted an open forum to increase awareness of the fact that an increasing number of young girls are suffering from eating disorders.

Meanwhile, Aspel said, if parents suspect their child has an eating disorder, they need to talk to their kids and get them help.

"Denial is a very strong factor," Aspel said. "You don't want to believe your child has a major problem such as that."

But sometimes, you have to face facts.

Affecting the Whole Family

This is the kind of advice Allison's mom wishes she'd had last summer. Allison's weight loss and dieting was affecting the entire family. Her parents argued over what was normal and what wasn't, and how best to get Allison to eat. Her father would say, "This is ridiculous. I can't believe you're causing this family this kind of grief." Her brothers yelled at her for making their mother cry.

Allison, like many kids with eating disorders, felt out of control.

But the one thing she could still control was what she had to eat.

Allison, like most kids with eating disorders, come from what would be described as "good" families, Riggs said. But their families often get sucked into the whirlpool of concern and frustration with the disorder.

"It's a kind of power within your family," Riggs said. ". . . Everyone focuses on the kid's eating." Ultimately, she said, "it's a cry for help."

Allison's mom said she was relieved when she finally got an appointment with Riggs.

She figured they'd meet with Riggs and her daughter would get a physical, and then they'd arrange for nutrition counseling, personal counseling for Allison—maybe for the whole family—to help her get back on track.

She told Allison they'd take the day off school, head to the doctor's office in the morning, then hit the Providence Place mall to go shopping and have lunch—a much-needed girls' day out.

She was stunned to hear Riggs say that Allison needed to be hospitalized that day or risk dying at home that night.

"I felt like I got shot with a gun," her mom said.

On the flip side, she said, she wanted to hug Riggs. "I could just feel the sense of relief come over my body. . . . It was like, 'Thank God.'"

A Tough Recovery

Allison says she initially thought it would be cool to spend a couple of days in the hospital, since she'd get to skip school.

But it wasn't fun for long.

She was confined to her bed, hooked up to a cardiac monitor. She was told she had to eat, or she'd be force-fed through a tube in her nose. She wasn't allowed to use the bathroom, unless someone was there to monitor her. And the only people allowed to visit were her parents and her brothers, from 2 to 4 and 6 to 8 P.M.

She spent eight days in the hospital, then eight more days in "partial" care. Allison jokingly calls it "daycare."

Her mom dropped her off at the hospital at 7:30, so she could be monitored while she ate breakfast, lunch and two snacks. She'd also get weighed and see medical specialists and tutors. Then, her mom would pick her up around 4 P.M. for dinner and to sleep at home for the night.

Allison's mom says the hospital staff was great, as were the teachers and other officials at her child's suburban middle school.

In fact, two of Allison's teachers and an assistant principal confided that their own daughters were struggling with eating disorders.

She says she's heard that 1 in 100 kids has an eating disorder, whether or not it's diagnosed. "You don't know how prevalent this is," she said.

Now that Allison is home, she's still regularly meeting with Riggs to monitor her progress. But instead of meeting with Aspel each week, she now meets every other week.

Allison is now doing great, her mom says. But she's still got a long way to go. She's had a peanut butter sandwich or two, and she's had a couple of Skittles as well.

But she needs to become more flexible about what she eats, and she needs to consume 3,000 calories a day to allow her body to grow naturally.

Allison, now a slim, pretty 12-year-old with long brown hair and a mouth full of braces, says she's open with her friends about what happened. "I told them I wasn't eating enough. I had an eating disorder, and my heart rate got so low I was hospitalized."

So she sits here now, in the sunroom of her suburban home, munching graham crackers and pudding, on the road to recovery.

But there's no quick fix to eating disorders, Riggs noted. "It's important that people not think of this as like strep throat—take amoxicyllin and it's over. This illness is chronic. [It requires] long-time treatment."

NOT FOR GIRLS ONLY: BOYS WITH EATING DISORDERS

Laura Pappano

Although eating disorders are commonly considered to be a female problem, Laura Pappano explains in the following selection that teenage boys can also suffer from disordered eating behavior. Experts estimate that men represent approximately 10 percent of all cases of eating disorders, she reports, while many more boys and young men suffer from eating problems that are less serious but still harmful. Unrealistic media images and shifting expectations concerning the ideal masculine body may be contributing to the upswing in eating disorders among males, the author notes. In addition, Pappano states, the challenge of dealing with stressful life changes and emotional problems can lead teenage boys and young men to develop eating disorders. Pappano is a staff writer for the *Boston Globe*.

At first, it was about getting a date. Jared Epps was a sophomore in high school when he noticed that the girl who caught his eye liked "really thin guys."

So in the spring, just as he was turning 16, Jared decided to lose weight. But what began as a mission to slim down soon became a secret, painful battle with food. He became obsessive about calorie counting, keeping a running tally of the day's intake on a scrap of paper, and exercised compulsively. According to his mother, Janice, he developed "weird eating habits." She describes seeing her teenage son limit himself to a lunch of three apples and some shredded wheat or a bag of carrots. When his sister, Jody, came home from college she was instantly alarmed: Jared, five feet six inches, had dropped from 147 to 126 pounds in six months.

Still, Jared wasn't satisfied. If only he were thinner, he remembers thinking, maybe he would feel more confident, more outgoing. Maybe that girl would notice. When he left for summer camp, he began "a kind of game with myself. Every day I would eat less and less." An apple and a yogurt for breakfast one day was reduced to an

Laura Pappano, "Every Day I Would Eat Less and Less," *Good Housekeeping*, vol. 23, August 2000, p. 116. Copyright © 2000 by Laura Pappano. Reproduced by permission.

apple and half a yogurt the next. He would slip out at night or during social events to run. By summer's end, he was running four and a half miles a day and consuming less than 500 calories—behavior typical of anorexics, who deny themselves food and exercise to excess. He came home weighing 112 pounds.

"He started losing muscle mass," recalls his father, Jimmy, sitting in the living room of the family's Salem, New Hampshire, home. "You would touch his shoulder and feel bone."

Worried, his mother brought Jared to the doctor. "I was expecting the doctor to say, 'Boy, that's a lot of weight you've lost. What's happening?' But," Janice says, "he didn't even question it." When she brought it up, she says, the doctor dismissed her concerns.

Not Just a Women's Problem

Traditionally considered a women's problem, eating disorders are now being diagnosed more frequently among young men. Some 8 million Americans suffer from these disorders. Conservative estimates suggest that one sufferer in ten is male, although some experts put the number as high as one in six. All agree that uncounted young men have eating problems that are less serious but still physically and emotionally destructive.

The obsession with weight loss and a fear of food are all too familiar to Dan Fox, an 18-year-old high school senior. As he sits in the den of his family's home in Sterling, Massachusetts, Dan, a straight-A student and aspiring film director, quietly describes his two-year struggle with anorexia. He has been hospitalized a half dozen times, he says, sometimes for weeks at a stretch.

As a child, Dan was teased for being "on the chubby side" and he began to equate thinness with happiness: "I can just remember being unhappy, and I figured I had seen people who were skinny and good-looking, and no one like that was ever unhappy."

At one point, Dan was running ten miles and eating just one bowl of cereal a day. Even after his weight fell so low that he was prohibited from running, he would jog in his room, back and forth, for an hour after everyone in his family had gone to bed. His health was so precarious he had to be weighed and have his vital signs checked several times a week.

His doctor, Richard C. Antonelli, M.D., says that even though Dan would claim to feel perfectly fine, the eating disorder was jeopardizing his life. His pulse rate was very low—in the mid-40s when it should have been 70 to 85 beats per minute. And the lack of protein in his diet was causing his body to break down its own proteins, weakening his heart and putting him at risk for heart failure.

"I was very concerned about Dan," says Dr. Antonelli, assistant professor of pediatrics at the University of Massachusetts Medical Center in Worcester. According to Dr. Antonelli, Dan, like many other anorexics, was in denial: "It was very difficult, initially, for him to recognize he had a problem."

Unlike Jared, who knew he needed help, Dan was angry with doctors who put him in the hospital and insisted he eat. But, after repeated hospitalizations and being rushed to the intensive care unit on one occasion, Dan eventually was able to see that something was terribly wrong. With the help of psychotherapy and medication, Dan is now trying to put the disorder behind him. He shows off his basement hangout, where he and friends play pool and Nintendo, and listen to music. He points to a photo of himself with his girlfriend at the junior prom. He has plans for college—and for his life. But he realizes he has a long way to go.

"I just want to be able to eat normally," he says. Although he eats three meals a day, he is so rigid about his diet that it is difficult for him to eat anywhere but at home. Typically he will eat two bowls of cereal with skim milk for breakfast, turkey with soy organic cheese on pita bread for lunch, and small portions of spaghetti, chicken or beef for dinner. "All junk food I am scared of. I don't eat anything fried," he says. Eventually, he adds, he'd love to just be out during the day and "be able to stop someplace and eat something."

Unrealistic Expectations

Experts say there is no easy way to explain why young men develop eating disorders. But some of them point to the powerful messages from the mass media on physical appearance. Girls have long been influenced by unrealistic images, ranging from the slim yet buxom Barbie doll to waif-thin model Kate Moss; now boys seem to be finding their own equivalents. "The physical standards are becoming just as impossible for men as they are for women," says Arnold Andersen, M.D., one of the nation's experts on male eating disorders.

The new male standard is a svelte body with clearly articulated muscles. It can be seen in ads, on TV, in the movies, in video games, even in children's toys. That image is taking a toll. Dr. Andersen, director of the eating disorders program at the University of Iowa College of Medicine, says his latest research on boys reveals that some 80 percent are dissatisfied with their bodies: "Half want to bulk up, and half want to lose."

Changes in the Masculine Ideal

At McLean Hospital in Belmont, Massachusetts, researcher Harrison Pope, M.D., empties plastic action figures onto a coffee table in his office. Dr. Pope, a psychiatry professor at Harvard Medical School, lines up three G.I. Joes—designed in 1964, the mid-1970s, and in 1992, respectively. His point is easy to see: The 1964 G.I. Joe looks like a trim, regular guy. The mid-'70s G.I. Joe is more muscular. And the newest model? Dr. Pope points out the rippled muscle, the "six-pack" of perfectly sculpted abdominals. "Not only is the modern Joe more muscular, he's leaner," Dr. Pope observes.

Of course, few young men are consciously trying to emulate plastic action figures. But the figures do underscore the shift in the masculine ideal, says Dr. Pope, coauthor with Katharine Phillips and Roberto Olivardia of *The Adonis Complex: The Secret Crisis of Male Body Obsession.*

The preoccupation with physical appearance is filtering down to elementary schools, where experts see more pressure on boys at frighteningly young ages. "Not only do I hear of first- and second-grade girls coming home and asking, 'Mommy, am I too fat?' but now I hear third, fourth, and fifth grade boys saying, 'Am I buff?'" says Catherine Steiner-Adair, Ed.D., director of education, prevention, and outreach at the Harvard Eating Disorders Center in Boston and a clinical and consulting psychologist. Steiner-Adair says middle school boys "actually think seriously about working out and weight lifting for body sculpting purposes."

The Quest for a Perfect Body

For 22-year-old Matt Berkeley, teased for being overweight from the time he was nine years old, the images of lean, muscular bodies in magazines such as *Men's Fitness*, *Flex*, and *Men's Health*, were impossible to resist. He wanted to look like that too. "I was amazed that the human physique could be so shaped, so symmetrical," recalls Matt, who lives in Waltham, Massachusetts. "I would see these guys with these perfect physiques, and it just motivated me toward my goal."

Matt began his quest for such a body after graduating from high school. "I did a whole makeover of myself," he says. He began simply enough, exercising regularly and watching what he ate. But it wasn't long before he was lifting weights two and a half hours a day, six or seven days a week. "The exercise was very addictive," he says. "Muscles were popping out everywhere; I was losing body fat."

But Matt wanted more. He read books on training and on food supplements—books with sometimes dangerous prescriptions for bulking up and losing fat. "I learned about how ephedrine [mixed with other drugs] can have synergistic effects for fat-burning," he says. Ephedrine is an ingredient in some nutritional supplements available at health-food and other stores. It can raise blood pressure, cause insomnia, and even lead to stroke.

Matt limited his food intake to exactly 1,600 calories a day—the amount he could burn off at the gym. He took ephedrine, often several times a day. His weight, once 185 pounds on his five-foot-eight-inch frame, dropped to 138 pounds. His waist shrank from 33 inches to 29 inches.

Fortunately for Matt, his drastic weight loss was only temporary. Although never formally diagnosed with an eating disorder, he realized something was wrong. He began psychotherapy. He enrolled in a community college and started thinking about his future. A relationship with a girlfriend blossomed.

He pulled himself out of his destructive cycle, cutting out ephedrine and eating whenever he was hungry. "After that, I was basically home free," says Matt, now 185 pounds and fit. "I finally accepted myself the way I was. I still try to better myself, but I don't go to extremes."

Triggering Male Eating Disorders

Mass media images aside, experts say male eating disorders are often part of a larger web of troubles that often includes depression. "You will never find one thing that is the original source," says Laura Goodman, a psychotherapist in private practice and author of *Is Your Child Dying to Be Thin?* "These disorders are not illnesses, but coping mechanisms—faulty ones."

For boys suffering from bulimia or binge eating disorder, Goodman says, food serves as a tool for dealing with suppressed emotions. Bulimics consume large amounts of food and then "purge" by exercising excessively, using laxatives or vomiting, or fasting between binges. The binge eater consumes food uncontrollably, but doesn't purge. Like anorexia, bulimia and binge eating can cause serious health problems, from mood swings to osteoporosis, kidney failure, heart failure, even death.

Boys with bulimia treat food as "their drug of choice," Goodman says, "stuffing negative feelings down in the body. When they throw up the food, they throw up the feelings." By contrast, anorexics, who often deny themselves food, find that eating may be the one thing in their lives they can actually control.

Some studies point to the challenge of coping with emerging sexuality as the stress point that triggers a disorder. David Herzog, M.D., president of the Harvard Eating Disorders Center, says boys are most likely to develop eating disorders around puberty or a few years later, when they prepare to leave home for college. Other research suggests there may be higher rates of eating disorders among gay males.

Research also points to a link between eating disorders and participation in sports such as wrestling, swimming, gymnastics, or running, in which a lower weight—or, alternatively, a bulkier build—may be a competitive advantage. In 1997, three college wrestlers exercised (and dehydrated) themselves to death trying to lose weight in order to compete in lower weight classes.

The seeds of eating disorders may be planted early and innocently when children turn to food to make themselves feel better. "There are a lot of kids who come home to an empty house and, until Mom or Dad gets there, find comfort in food," Goodman says. "That can be a precursor to an eating disorder."

Children who are encouraged to diet are also at greater risk, experts say; they emphasize that weight issues in youngsters should be tackled through healthy eating and regular exercise.

Struggling to Recover

Jared Epps found that once he started losing weight, it was hard to stop. "Every time I looked in the mirror, I thought, I could definitely lose this or I could definitely lose that," he says, pinching his waist in a mock gesture. Food became so threatening that Jared would avoid social events where he would have to eat—or he would lie and say he'd already eaten.

Jared, 19, continues to work on his recovery and credits his psychotherapist with helping him in his continuing effort to recover from anorexia. He looks healthy and estimates his weight at 150 pounds, though he is not certain because he no longer weighs himself. He eats, but confines himself to a limited diet. And he still struggles to eat in public, preferring to have his meals alone.

"I think it would be great if I could have a meal and not think, How many calories does this have? or Should I go exercise?" he says. "A goal for me is to go out with friends and eat and not think more about the food than about the conversation we are having."

THE GROWING NUMBER OF ADULT MEN WITH EATING DISORDERS

Lisa Liddane

Lisa Liddane is a group fitness instructor and a staff writer for the *Orange County Register*, a California newspaper. In the following selection, Liddane reveals that an increasing number of adult men suffer from eating disorders such as bulimia and anorexia. Furthermore, she writes, men are particularly susceptible to body dysmorphia disorder. As the author explains, men with this disorder believe that they are too skinny; they work out obsessively in order to build muscle, and they sometimes begin to abuse steroids. Men with eating disorders often have difficulty finding support and treatment because of the common misconception that such conditions only occur among women, Liddane points out. In addition, she reports, guilt and shame may prevent many men from admitting that they have a problem and seeking the treatment they need.

The secret signs of bulimia and anorexia are familiar. Looking in the mirror and always seeing an unfit, unattractive, fat person—even when the real reflection isn't. Purging in the restroom after eating dinner with friends. Starving oneself by eating only one meal a day. Thinking constantly about one's body.

But the person in the mirror is not familiar.

It's a man.

His name is Dick. The 32-year-old sales associate from Anaheim, California, asked that his last name not be used. None of his family members, friends and co-workers know that he has been struggling for more than a decade with a distorted body image.

Dick is among a growing number of men—about one million in the United States, by most estimates—who battle with what is still largely perceived as a woman's mental-health condition. The number of men with eating disorders might be greater—from 3 million to 5 million, said Roberto Olivardia, clinical psychologist at McLean Hospital in Belmont, Mass., and co-author of *The Adonis Complex: The Secret Crisis of Male Body Obsession.*

Male eating disorders are underdiagnosed because society lacks awareness of them and men are less likely to admit they have this medical problem and seek help, Olivardia said.

That's changing slowly, he added.

Knowing who might be at risk could help prevent eating disorders from developing, body-image researchers say. Understanding the nature of male body obsession and eating disorders might help men recognize that they have these conditions and seek treatment.

Eating Disorders in Men

Doctors and psychologists do not know the exact causes of distorted body images and eating disorders in men, because research in these areas is in the infancy stages.

But more studies on men and boys are emerging in medical publications such as the *International Journal of Eating Disorders Research.*

One in six men might have anorexia and bulimia, according to a 1999 study in *Psychiatric Annals*, by Dr. Arnold E. Andersen, an eating-disorder researcher at University of Iowa.

Andersen classifies at-risk men into four groups:
- Men in sports and athletic activities who need to control weight for performance. This is the most prevalent group.
- Men who were overweight or obese and had negative, sometimes traumatic experiences related to their weight.
- Men whose fathers had ill health, possibly weight-related, and possibly died because of it.
- Men who want to improve their body image.

Researchers have coined a term for one type of male body obsession: body dysmorphia disorder (BDD). An example of BDD is muscle dysmorphia, sometimes called "reverse anorexia" or "biggerexia." This disorder occurs when normal-size or big, muscular men think of themselves as thin and scrawny. Some men with muscle dysmorphia could be workout-aholics, or users of steroids or muscle-enhancing supplements.

Researchers also know that the effects of eating disorders on men are similar to those on women: weakened, fragile bones, elevated risk for heart attacks because of electrolyte imbalance, tooth decay, gastrointestinal problems and damage to the esophagus.

Causes of Male Eating Disorders

One theory in research that is gaining ground is the genetic link. Scientists suspect that the predisposition to an eating disorder can run in some families and in both sexes.

But genes aren't the only factors to blame. In the past decade, magazines such as *Men's Health* have perpetuated the myth that the look of male health is lean, low in fat, with Michelangelo-chiseled musculature, said Lynne Luciano, author of *Looking Good: Male Body Image in*

America. Luciano is assistant professor of history at University of California, Dominguez Hills.

Lean and muscular physiques also are glorified in sports, TV, movies, music videos and advertising. They're even in toys. If GI Joe Extreme (the enhanced version of the action figure) was life-size, Luciano said, he would have a 32-inch waist, 44-inch chest and impossible 32-inch biceps.

The danger of these images, Olivardia said, is they create a blueprint for the masculine man that is difficult for most men to follow without resorting to drastic, unhealthy measures, such as taking steroids and muscle-enhancing supplements, using laxatives, working out obsessively, and becoming anorexic and/or bulimic.

Distorted body images and eating disorders are often the manifestation of other problems, Olivardia said. Low self-esteem in childhood, adolescence and adulthood, and psychological, emotional and mental issues can drive men to focus on their body or specific parts (such as the midsection) and see themselves as physically flawed.

Some people with a history of obsessive behaviors carry these over into their eating habits as a form of control, said Sarah Steinmeyer, psychologist at South Coast Medical Center Eating Disorders Program in Laguna Beach, California.

"Eating disorders are rarely about food," she said. "Food is a metaphor for other aspects of life. A man with an eating disorder and body obsession sometimes thinks he can control food, but food actually controls him."

Terry Murphy, 53, loathes what he sees when he looks in the mirror—an out-of-shape, overweight man. At 6 feet and 210 pounds, the management consultant said he feels he has no control over his body and is depressed about it.

"I can't get it out of my mind," Murphy said. "I think about it at least a dozen times a day."

Murphy, who said he never had weight issues before, put on pounds over the years when a heart condition prevented him from maintaining six-day-a-week, 90-minute intense workouts. Murphy continues to exercise most days of the week, but has reduced the intensity for the sake of his heart.

So he diets. His breakfast: a regular-size beef patty and cottage cheese. Lunch consists of a protein drink and a banana or an apple. Dinner is a low-calorie salad with chicken, half a glass of milk and the occasional small cookie.

Going to Dieting Extremes

Dick, like Murphy, feels frustrated and alone.

"Ever since I can remember, my physical appearance has been a way of gauging my self-worth," Dick said.

Dick's weight for most of his teens was normal, but when he turned

19, he gained weight. At 5 feet, 6 inches, he weighed 195 pounds. After a routine physical exam, the doctor told him he was obese.

To lose weight, Dick did several things. He starved himself in private. And when he ate out with friends, he consumed a normal amount of food. But shortly after, he would excuse himself from the table, go to the public restroom and make himself vomit. "The sooner I could purge, the easier it would be to get the food out," he said.

He exercised relentlessly most days of the week, sometimes more than once a day.

Within a year, he lost 40 pounds.

Dick knew what he was doing was not healthy. But he kept it a secret. He was ashamed to talk about it with anyone. "It's a girl's disease," he said.

In 1989, a roommate caught him purging. At the friend's urging, he found a doctor who treated eating disorders. "The doctor tried to scare me with statistics and stories of girls who had died because of ruptures to their esophagus. I went three times for regular counseling. And then, I stopped. I thought I could do this on my own."

And he stopped bulimic behavior for six years. His weight stabilized at about 155 pounds. But his esophagus had been damaged from years of regurgitating food.

After a painful divorce several years ago, Dick returned to some unhealthy behaviors.

He has nothing but coffee throughout the day. His only meal is at night.

"I don't know that I'm over it," he said.

Less Support Available for Men

Dick has tried to look for men's support groups—to no avail. He does not feel comfortable attending women's anorexia and bulimia groups. "That happens fairly often to men who are trying to get help," Steinmeyer said. "And that's terrible, because the lack of support groups for men only perpetuates the myth that this is only a woman's disease."

When men seek help they are in the advanced stages of their eating disorders, because it takes them a long time to recognize and admit that they have a serious health problem and to develop the courage to communicate their need for help, said Jane Supino, executive director for the Center for the Study of Anorexia and Bulimia in New York.

Treatments for men are the same as women's—they are tailored to the individual. They vary from outpatient visits to hospital confinement for days, weeks or months. They might include intense nutritional intervention, such as intravenous feeding, if needed. Olivardia said treatment programs that target the problems from many angles with a team approach—involving the primary doctor, a psychologist or psychiatrist, a nutritionist and support groups—are likely to have the best results.

Dying to Win: Athletes and Eating Disorders

Joel Hood

In the article that follows, Joel Hood discusses the prevalence of disordered eating among female athletes in high school and college. According to experts, he explains, eating disorders occur ten times more often among female athletes than among women in the general population. Women who participate in sports such as gymnastics or track and field—where smaller and lighter athletes are believed to have a competitive advantage—are particularly at risk for developing an eating disorder, Hood reveals. Researchers suggest that the self-discipline and obsessive drive to win that enable athletes to succeed may also make them more likely to develop the compulsive behaviors associated with eating disorders. Hood reports that eating disorders have reached a crisis level in college sports, but few schools or coaches are equipped to recognize the signs of anorexia or bulimia among their top athletes. Hood is a staff writer for the *Modesto Bee*, a California newspaper.

Rock bottom wasn't how she imagined it. It was worse.

Sure, on the way there she confronted debilitating levels of shame, fear and self-loathing. She endured lengthy hospital stays and countless support groups. She revealed to others the kind of intimate details of her life it hurt to remember, much less speak aloud.

But rock bottom was deeper still.

It was beyond those memories she carried of stuffing herself with food in front of her friends, hoping to silence their needling glares once and for all.

It was past visions she had of crying herself to sleep at night in her room, wishing someone—anyone!—might hear her muffled pleas for help.

At the absolute bottom of this disease that tormented her, as well as millions of other young athletes, there were no images to draw upon, just a series of painful questions:

How long can I keep this a secret?

Could I stop if I needed to?

I know I'm killing myself—does that mean I'm suicidal?

How did I get here?

Julie, a former Stanislaus District, California, athlete who asked that her real name not be revealed, hit rock bottom when, even after repeated visits with counselors to treat her eating disorder, she realized she had no answers for those questions and simply stopped caring if her illness killed her.

At 16, Julie had given up on life. At least, life as she knew it.

"When it started, this was just something I was going to do for a while to keep my weight down," she said. "It just spiraled out of control and I ended up in the hospital and almost dying because of it.

"It took over my life."

A Problem for Athletes

Julie is not alone in her struggle to combat an eating disorder.

Despite an increase in public awareness, despite efforts by the National Collegiate Athletic Association (NCAA) and California's high school athletic governing body to inform coaches and administrators of the dangers of starvation and malnutrition, doctors say eating disorders like anorexia nervosa and bulimia continue to rise among college and high school athletes.

This is particularly true among female athletes in cross country, track and field, volleyball, gymnastics and figure skating, sports that generally demand lower percentages of body fat to excel.

Statistics released by the National Collegiate Athletic Association in a 1999 study show female athletes are 10 times as likely to develop eating disorders than women in the general population. According to the National Center for Health, about one in every 100 adolescent women between the ages of 10 and 20 are affected.

And despite a notable increase in the number of male athletes who are anorexic or bulimic, statistics show the problem among females is still significantly higher, primarily due to insecurities about body image and the increased visibility of women's athletics in society.

Frequently, it seems, the same drive and discipline that makes a champion athlete also allows him or her to fall prey to eating disorders.

"The problem of anorexia (in athletics) is worse today," said Dr. Craig Johnson, Director of Eating Disorders Program at Laureate Psychiatric Hospital in Tulsa, Okla., who led the NCAA's 1999 study. "Anorexia is an obsession and a compulsiveness to continue to lose weight regardless of the weight the person is at. The drive to lose weight is relentless."

Julie was a standout distance runner in high school, one of the area's best in cross country and track beginning her freshman year. It was her competitiveness that drove her to be the best, she said.

Like many, Julie's eating disorder started innocently. Trying to streamline her already slim physique, she occasionally skipped lunch on busy afternoons during her freshman year in 1998–99. Sometimes she'd leave home without eating breakfast.

Other days, when she felt too full after eating or when the pressure to do well in an upcoming meet became too great, she'd discreetly sneak off to the bathroom at school and force herself to throw up by sticking her finger down her throat.

This wasn't something she was seriously concerned about and she believed there was no need to alarm anyone by telling her coaches or family about it.

It just made sense to her that if she were lighter, she'd be faster.

But by track season of her sophomore year, her eating disorder had worsened to the point that Julie was forcing herself to throw up on a daily basis: at home, at school, on race days, it didn't matter.

Eventually, Julie's on-field production had slipped far enough that she was a middle-of-the-pack runner.

Her coaches were puzzled, but their solution, Julie said, was to focus harder during training.

That's what Julie did, but by the summer before her junior year she had dropped extreme amounts of weight and found herself tiring easily at practice. After she weighed more than 100 pounds as a freshman, the 5-foot-4 Julie had fallen to 78 pounds that summer. And her weakened condition, combined with the intense Central Valley heat, made her solo training runs a deadly risk.

One hot day in July 2000, as she prepared to enter her junior year of high school, Julie collapsed and nearly passed out while on a solo training run. It was then that Julie first realized the dangers of what she was doing. Later that day, she told her mom about her eating disorder.

And as the summer drew to a close, a teary-eyed Julie worked up enough courage to tell her cross country coach about it. Julie had no choice but to quit the team.

"That was one of the toughest things I've ever done," she said.

Life-Threatening Effects

Although often used as synonyms when describing a person with an eating disorder, anorexia and bulimia are quite different.

Anorexia refers to someone who consistently tries to shed weight, regardless of height, weight or body shape. Most anorexics force themselves to skip meals, trying to get by on as little food as possible during the day.

Bulimics usually allow themselves to eat whatever they want, but then throw it up. Most classic "binge-and-purge" eaters are bulimic, according to Anorexia Nervosa and Related Eating Disorders Inc., a nonprofit organization affiliated with the National Eating Disorders Association.

Short- and long-term health problems can include the loss of menstruation, urinary tract infections, irregular heartbeats and damage to the colon and kidneys. It also can begin the process of osteoporosis, the loss of bone mass, at an early age.

At its worst, it can lead to death. Complications of the disorder include cardiac arrest or electrolyte imbalance, and suicide, according the National Institute of Mental Health.

Women are more susceptible to eating disorders than men for a variety of physical and psychological reasons.

In general, women's bodies have more fatty tissue and less lean muscle than men's, contributing to a slower metabolic rate. That makes it more difficult for women to drop weight and keep it off during exercising.

But that's only part of the equation.

Some athletes, and coaches, mistakenly believe the lower a person's body fat percentage, the greater their chances for athletic success. Insecurities about body image, more so for women than men, and stress to perform athletically also contribute significantly.

After more than a year of counseling and visits with doctors, Julie felt her drive to become a better runner and the pressures of school were at the root of her anorexia and bulimia.

"I was always wanting to do the best," Julie said. "I always trained like crazy, so it would have been tough for my coaches to see that there was something wrong."

Kim Duyst, Stanislaus State's longtime cross country and track and field coach, said that's more common than one might think.

"These are overachievers, they are very disciplined people," Duyst said. "Having to juggle school work with things like weight training and practice schedules, combined with the pressures to perform at a high level athletically, it's easy to see how they can fall into a routine of not eating properly."

That Slender Look

Body image can also have an impact. Athletes, even those in top physical condition, are influenced by the images of slender runners and other athletes who adorn the glossy covers of magazines and appear on television: lean body mass, healthy-looking and fit, always with a smile on their face.

In subjectively judged sports like gymnastics and figure skating, the pressure to look a certain way can be even greater. In a 1995 report released by U.S.A. Gymnastics, the sport's national governing body, it was discovered that female gymnasts perceive that having a body type similar to that of the existing champion would increase their chances at becoming one themselves.

According to the NCAA, the female U.S. gymnastics team in 1972 had an average height of 5-foot-3 and an average weight of 106 pounds.

In 1992, the average height was 4-9 and the average weight was 83 pounds.

The study determined that in judged sports, an athlete will sometimes channel her anxiety into exercising strict control over her body size and image. That same study reported that 62 percent of NCAA gymnasts surveyed had disordered eating habits.

"I tell the parents of the kids I coach not to make a real big deal about the weight issue," said Paul Mayer, owner of Gymnastics Unlimited in Modesto and Turlock, California. "A lot of times, the image (an athlete) has of herself is not what the rest of us see."

Severe weight loss can also be driven by the skimpy clothing athletes are forced to wear in their sport, coaches say. In sports like volleyball and cross country, where the athletes wear little more than lycra underwear, the struggle to maintain a thin appearance can create life-threatening circumstances.

"The kids are basically wearing colored underwear," Sonora High volleyball coach Darla Mayhew said. "And it seems like (the uniforms) are getting shorter every year."

Crisis Stage in the NCAA

The NCAA completed a study in 1999 that shows the problem at the collegiate level has reached a crisis stage.

In the 1999 study that looked at athletes with eating disorders at elite Division I universities, the NCAA discovered that nearly 14 percent of female athletes had "clinically significant problems" when it came to weight loss and that 34 percent were at risk for developing eating disorders.

The NCAA's study concludes that female athletes "consistently reported higher rates of disordered eating behaviors" due, in part, to significantly lower self-esteem than male athletes.

Disturbingly, the NCAA's research found the percentage of body fat that college-age female athletes desired most would result in health problems.

Because this was the first study of its kind by the NCAA, it's difficult to determine if that's a significant change from 10 or 20 years ago.

There has never been a comprehensive study on the number of statewide high school athletes afflicted with eating disorders, according to the California Interscholastic Federation (CIF), the state's governing body for high school sports.

Keeping Things Private

Athletes are generally reluctant to talk about disordered eating habits, often leaving coaches, parents, athletic trainers and friends to wonder privately about a distance runner who looks like she's losing large amounts of weight or a setter on the volleyball team who seems lethargic at practice.

That's one of the reasons why it's difficult sometimes to determine which athletes are suffering an eating disorder and which are simply dedicating themselves to a strict workout regimen and diet.

Julie said she resisted telling her coaches about her eating disorder until it was clear to her that she had lost control of it.

"I remember thinking to myself, 'This is going to kill me. But I'm going to die sometime, I might as well go out now,'" she said. "I was pretty much suicidal at that point."

All but one of the nine high school and collegiate coaches contacted by *The Modesto Bee* for this story said they believed they had coached an athlete who was anorexic or bulimic. And each of them stressed how difficult it is to monitor their athletes' behaviors away from school or competition.

"As a coach, you're really handcuffed in that situation," said one area coach who asked not to be identified. "In the case (of eating disorders), there aren't a lot of tell-tale signs you can point to until the athlete gets to a real severe stage. You don't know if it's the flu or another illness. If the athlete isn't willing to talk to you about it, you simply don't know what the problem is. But you can't ignore it."

Unfortunately, coaches are generally forced to police the problem themselves. And as long as that athlete is performing at a high level on the field, coaches are often reluctant to call attention to their concerns.

"As a coach of an athlete who you think might have a problem, your main obligation is to get help," Duyst said. "But unfortunately, coaches don't always know what to do in that situation. And in some cases, they don't want to ask an athlete about a problem because they're afraid what the answer might be."

No Easy Solution

Searching for answers, the NCAA increased its efforts to inform coaches, athletic directors and trainers about the dangers of eating disorders in the forms of posters, videos and literature sent to member schools.

Still, after meeting with a student-athlete advisory council in 2001, NCAA officials determined the information was not getting to those who most needed it—the athletes. As a result, the NCAA created a more comprehensive look at eating disorders and information on nutrition and health on its Web site at www.ncaa.org.

But information is all the NCAA and CIF can provide. Until more of their member schools recognize the crisis, the organizations aren't in a position to create and enforce rules that might help athletes curb their eating disorders, said Randy Dick, the Senior Assistant Director of Injury Surveillance for the NCAA.

For example, since 1996, the University of Tulsa has forced each incoming athlete (either freshman or junior college transfer) to take a test about their eating habits, with the hope of identifying athletes who may fall prey to eating disorders.

But only a small handful of schools have this type of screening process, Johnson said. The NCAA has no power to force schools to adopt one, Dick said.

"We're trying to get information to the schools about what they should be aware of," Dick said. "But that's all we can really do."

An Enduring Battle

After quitting the cross country team in her junior year in 2001, Julie left school and began independent study at home. There, even though her mother was on hand to closely monitor her eating habits and she had regularly scheduled meetings with counselors, Julie's eating disorder worsened.

By then she understood her sickness but said she was not psychologically prepared to fight it. She was eating more, which meant she had to throw up more often.

One evening during her junior year, Julie was at home when she dropped to her knees with severe stomach pains and began spitting up blood. After being rushed to the emergency room, Julie had to be fed intravenously because she would not eat the hospital food.

"It's pretty horrible because my mom was trying to help me, but I wasn't letting her," she said. "The way I was thinking was so screwed up. Even to this day, my mom probably doesn't know how bad it got.

"I used to sit by myself and cry and ask myself every day why I did this."

That was just more than a year ago.

She finished her high school education in April 2002 and has since enrolled full time in college, where she hopes to continue running competitively.

Julie is healthy and fit, but said it's still a daily fight to control her eating disorder. It's a battle she doesn't always win.

She admits to still purging occasionally and she has quit attending her group sessions. But mainly that's to focus on her schoolwork, she said.

Julie said she still keeps her illness private from everyone except certain members of her family and her closest friends. But one of those she makes sure to talk to is her younger sister, who is now a teen-ager.

"I don't tell her the methods I use because I don't want her to get involved in it," she said. "I'm afraid of her getting into it. I just want her to know what I've had to go through. I try not to lecture her about it because that didn't work for me. I took health classes in (high school).

"I knew what the dangers were and it didn't protect me."

CHAPTER 2

UNDERSTANDING EATING DISORDERS

THE BIOLOGICAL BASIS OF EATING DISORDERS

Emily Sohn

In the following selection, science writer Emily Sohn examines the possibility that there are genetic and biological causes behind the development of eating disorders. Research has revealed that eating disorders tend to run in families, she relates; for instance, studies of identical twins show that if one twin has an eating disorder, the other twin is much more likely to also develop an eating disorder. Researchers are discovering specific genes linked to eating disorders, Sohn reports, as well as evidence of hormonal and chemical imbalances that appear to play a role in eating disorders. Most insurance companies consider eating disorders to be a mental health problem, the author writes, so often they will not cover all the medical expenses related to treatment. However, Sohn points out, new evidence that eating disorders have a biological basis may lead to increased insurance coverage. Sohn has written for *U.S. News & World Report, New Scientist*, and *Science*.

Dinnertime was always stressful at the Corbett house. Every evening at 6 o'clock precisely, the five kids would take their assigned places at the table between Mom and Dad. Food was served family style, and whatever you took, you had to eat. You couldn't have dessert until after you had finished everything on your plate. "It was not a relaxing time to sit at the table and eat," recalls Cathie Reinard, 35, about her childhood in Rochester, N.Y. But the rigid rules just added to an underlying tension. As the kids got older, it became clear that most meals would end with Mom's excusing herself, going into the bathroom, and making herself throw up.

Messages about food were inconsistent and confusing to the Corbett kids, especially the three girls. On the one hand, dessert was served every night, and food was always part of family gatherings. On the other hand, the girls, all petite and athletic, were constantly being told they were fat—both by Mom at home and by their gymnastics coach, who wanted his athletes lean. Food was forbidden fruit. Between-meal

snacks were prohibited, and the padlock on the kitchen pantry kept little hands away from the candy, Pop-Tarts, and soda stashed inside.

With so many rules and restrictions, it's no wonder that all three
girls developed eating disorders, say the Corbetts, now grown and
with families of their own. Cathie started sticking her fingers down
her throat in high school, after a gymnastics injury prevented her
from working out. Her identical twin, Bonnie, developed anorexia in
college, dropping 50 pounds off her 5-foot, 120-pound frame in six
months. It began, she says, when a boyfriend pointed out her growing beer belly. Their older sister, Liz, 38, was an "exercise bulimic": To
make up for eating sprees, she repeatedly pushed her body to the
point of injury from daily workouts that could last for three hours or
more. Even their brother Daryl, 41, lost his appetite for a few months
when he broke up with his first girlfriend in college.

Their mother, Margery Bailey, still feels very guilty about her children's problems. And no wonder. When Bonnie was hospitalized with
anorexia at age 19 in 1985, Bailey says the doctors severely restricted
her visits. "I was told it was my fault."

Dysfunctional families are still a common target of blame, as is a
dysfunctional culture obsessed with thinness. But as doctors learn
more about eating disorders, it is becoming clear that genetics and
biology may be equally important causal factors for the estimated 5
million to 10 million Americans who struggle with anorexia, bulimia,
and binge-eating disorders. Although family and culture may provide
the ultimate trigger, it seems increasingly likely that hormones and
brain chemicals prime a certain group of people to push themselves
to starvation.

The Hidden Killer

Eating disorders are the deadliest of all psychiatric disorders, killing or
contributing to the deaths of thousands every year. An estimated
50,000 people currently suffering from an eating disorder will eventually die as a result of it. Anorexics, who pursue thinness so relentlessly
through diet and exercise that they drop to below 85 percent of ideal
body weight, often suffer heart attacks, arthritis, osteoporosis, and other
health problems. Bulimics eat uncontrollably, then compensate by
throwing up, taking laxatives, or exercising obsessively—behaviors that
can upset the body's chemical balance enough that it stops working.

As with depression and other serious psychiatric illnesses, eating disorders now appear to be a familial curse. Relatives of eating disorder
patients are 7 to 12 times as likely to develop an eating disorder as is
the general population, studies show. Depression, anxiety disorders,
and other related illnesses also appear more frequently in the same
families. That doesn't rule out a shared environment as a contributing
factor, says psychologist Michael Strober of the University of California-
Los Angeles. But, he adds, "anytime you see a disorder that runs in fam-

ilies, you begin to suspect some hereditary influence."

The women in Bailey's family have been fighting a losing battle with food for generations. When Bailey was 18, her 55-pound mother starved herself to death, sneaking laxatives in the hospital until the very end. Other relatives have also suffered from anorexia "I was always told I was fat and ugly and dumb," recalls Bailey, a 63-year-old retired nurse. She vividly remembers how she and her brothers secreted cans of food because they weren't getting enough to eat at meals. But, she concedes now, the sheer number of eating disorders in her family suggests something deeper going on.

A Powerful Obsession

Deadly eating disorders exist in cultures far removed from Hollywood and Madison Avenue and have been around far longer than glossy women's magazines. But if that weren't evidence enough for an underlying biology, the patients themselves are the first to say their eating disorders have a power far greater than peer pressure. Indeed, Stephanie Rose's illness had such a strong "personality" that she named it "Ed." It started with a diet to lose 8 pounds of weight gain after her freshman year of college. But her success became an obsession that landed her in the hospital nine times over the next four years. She crashed a car and a bicycle, both times after passing out from nutrient deprivation. She chugged bottles of poison-control syrup to make herself throw up, even if she had eaten only a bite of a tuna fish sandwich or a few grains of cereal. Even in the hospital, she shoved batteries in her underwear to fool the nurses when they weighed her. Talking and reading took too much energy, so she stared at the TV instead, gray-skinned, too weak to think.

At her sickest, the 5-foot, 5-inch Needham, Mass., resident weighed 75 pounds. She had a mild heart attack at age 21 as a result of her starved state. Doctors told her bluntly that she was going to die, and nurses sat with her 24 hours a day to make sure she didn't pull out her feeding tube. Now 29, fully recovered and happily married with a 15-month-old baby of her own, Rose can't believe she would flirt with death for arms that looked like toothpicks. "It was like someone took over my body," she says, "this guy, Ed."

The most convincing evidence for genetics comes from twins. If one twin has an eating disorder, the other is far more likely to have a similar illness if the twins are identical rather than fraternal. Since identical twins are genetic clones of each other, that is powerful evidence that genes play an important role, says psychiatrist Cynthia Bulik of Virginia Commonwealth University: "Until now, people would have said there wasn't a genetic effect in anorexia. And what we're saying is that there really is, and it's not minimal."

Several groups of researchers are now hunting for the specific genes involved in eating disorders, with some promising leads. The first two comprehensive scans of the human genome have recently turned up hot spots for anorexia-linked genes on several chromosomes, including Chromosome 1, which seems to harbor genes for the most severe form of anorexia. "We now know the location of several genes in the human genome which increase risk for anorexia nervosa," says University of Pennsylvania psychiatrist Wade Berrettini, a senior author of a study in the March 2002 issue of the *American Journal of Human Genetics*. "Prior to this, we did not." Other preliminary work is pointing to different areas of the genome that may be involved in bulimia, says psychiatrist Walter Kaye of the University of Pittsburgh.

None of the scientists exploring the genome expects to find easy answers or simple genetic switches. Indeed, hundreds of genes are already known to influence appetite and eating regulation in some way, a testament to how complex the eating impulse really is in the grand scheme of human biology.

But some patterns are emerging. The most obvious is that 90 percent of eating disorders occur in girls and women, most often beginning in adolescence. This clue has some experts exploring the genes that control hormone production. During the teen years in most girls, estrogen-producing genes kick in, triggering puberty. And there is evidence, says Michigan State psychologist Kelly Klump, suggesting that those genes may also contribute to eating disorders in some girls: Genes appear to be involved in 17-year-old twins with eating disorders but not in 11-year-old twins, who are mostly prepubescent. But even more striking, Klump says, a study of 11-year-old twins who had gone through puberty and exhibited warning signs of the illness showed the same genetic pattern as the 17-year-olds. Klump notes, by analogy, that depression hits girls twice as hard after puberty as before.

Hard-Wired in the Brain

Other researchers are linking eating disorders to personality traits that are hard-wired into the brain. Anorexics tend to be Type A—anxious, perfectionist, rigid. Those traits can translate into an unhealthy body image: When a driven perfectionist sets her mind on being slender, self-control can become a measure of success. Anorexics also tend to be ritualistic about the food they eat, cutting it into tiny pieces or eating only a specific type of food at only a specific time of day.

Such an obsessive temperament often appears to be inborn. In Kathryn Carvette DeVito's case, the first signs appeared at age 7. She started having panic attacks on the school playground and became preoccupied with getting her homework perfect, starting over and over again if necessary. Then she developed some classic symptoms of obsessive-compulsive disorder: "If I touched a doorknob 15 times, everything would be OK," she says. Kathryn hit puberty earlier than her classmates, and when a doctor told her she was heavier than the average sixth grader, her obsessions turned to food. She dropped to a low of 85 pounds before seeking help when she was 19. Even now, though the 5-foot, 2-inch Boston University senior sees a psychologist weekly and has stabilized her weight at about 100 pounds, she says that she sometimes eats as little as 100 calories a day. She works out every day and does sit-ups in her bed at night.

Brain chemicals may contribute to illnesses such as Kathryn's, says the University of Pittsburgh's Kaye. It may be that people who go on to develop the anxiety and obsessiveness associated with eating disorders have abnormally high levels of serotonin, one of the brain's major chemical messengers for mood, sexual desire, and food intake. Losing weight lowers serotonin, so anorexics may stop eating in a subconscious attempt to lower their uncomfortably high serotonin levels, says psychiatrist Evelyn Attia of the New York State Psychiatric Institute. But when a person stops eating, her brain churns out even more serotonin, Attia says. So, the anorexic gets caught "in a vicious cycle where the behavior tries to compensate for the uncomfortable feeling of biochemical imbalance but can never catch up."

Kaye also has evidence that the brains of recovered bulimics process serotonin in a way that is different from the brains of healthy people. It's not entirely clear yet if their brains were different before they developed the disease or if dieting caused the changes. Still, such chemical differences suggest that drugs like Prozac, used to treat depression and compulsive behaviors, might be helpful for treating eating disorders as well. In a small study, Kaye found that Prozac, which helps the brain's pathways work better, helped prevent relapses in recovered anorexics.

Cultural Influences

Despite all these biomedical advances in understanding eating disorders, victims still face a long and uncertain road to recovery. Only about half of anorexics and bulimics ever recover enough to maintain a healthy weight and positive self-image. Thirty percent of anorexics have residual symptoms that persist long into adulthood, and 1 in 10 cases remains chronic and unremitting. Without treatment, up to 20 percent of cases end in premature death.

Denial and resistance to treatment are fierce psychological obstacles once an eating disorder has taken hold, so scientists are looking more and more to prevention. And ironically, given the move away from cultural explanations for the disorders, the best interventions for now may still be psychosocial. Surveys show that 42 percent of children in first through third grade want to be thinner and that 81 percent of 10-year-olds are afraid of being fat. Those attitudes are clearly not genetic, and they are so pervasive that they could be pushing the genetically vulnerable over the edge. "If people never diet," Bulik says, "they might never enter into the higher-risk category for developing eating disorders."

One of the most striking examples of culture's influence comes from Fiji, where a bulky body has always been a beautiful body. Women on the South Pacific island have traditionally complimented one another for gaining weight. Food is starchy, calorie-dense, and plentiful. But when TV came to the island in 1995—with shows like *Melrose Place* and commercials celebrating thinness—the depictions of beauty radically altered Fijians' self-image—especially the girls'. According to a study published in June 2002 by Harvard psychiatrist and anthropologist Anne Becker, by 1998 the proportion of girls at risk for developing eating disorders more than doubled to 29 percent of the population. The percentage of girls who vomited to lose weight jumped from zero to 11 percent. "We actually talked to girls who explicitly said, 'I want to be thin because I watch TV, and everyone on TV has all those things, and they're thin,'" Becker says. Likewise, non-Western immigrants to the United States are more likely to develop eating disorders than are their relatives in the homeland.

The Cost of Starvation

While scientists debate and explore the causes of eating disorders, victims and their families are being hard hit financially. Hospitalization and around-the-clock care to revive a starving patient can cost more than $1,000 a day. Full recovery can take years of therapy, often involving the whole family. But because eating disorders are classified as a mental illness, insurance plans rarely cover the full costs of treatment. Kitty Westin slammed into just that painful wall. Her daughter Anna had struggled with anorexia as a teenager but seemed healthy when she came home to Chaska, Minn., after her sophomore year at the University of Oregon in Eugene. Within months, depression and anxiety again consumed Anna. She couldn't sleep. She withdrew from her family and friends. She stopped eating and spent hours at the gym every day. By summer's end, Anna, who had always been petite, could barely stand without feeling dizzy. At 5 feet, 4 inches, she weighed 82 pounds, and her vital signs were dangerously low. No matter how hard she fought the anorexia, she felt powerless. "It won't leave me alone," she told her mother.

For the next six months, Anna checked in and out of the hospital. She would improve as an inpatient. But as soon as she went home, she'd get sick again, says Kitty Westin, who quit her job as a psychologist to take care of her daughter. The family's health insurance company, Blue Cross and Blue Shield of Minnesota, refused to fully cover the costs of residential treatment, leaving the family to pay for whatever they could. On Feb. 17, 2000, worn out from her struggle, Anna killed herself. She was 21. Her mother, now a full-time advocate for better insurance coverage, says the family's battles with the insurance company exacerbated Anna's illness. "See, I'm not sick," Anna would say. "The insurance company says I'm not sick."

A Real Medical Illness

Such attitudes are slowly changing. In June 2001 the state of Minnesota settled a lawsuit against Blue Cross for repeatedly denying coverage to children with mental health problems. The settlement required the company to pay the state $8.2 million for treating families that had been refused coverage. The company is also becoming more accountable to eating disorder patients via an appointed, independent three-member panel that must review mental health appeals soon after receiving them. Westin is convinced that such a process would have saved Anna's life. "There is no doubt in my mind," she says, "that a panel would have reversed the [insurance company's] decision."

A legal acknowledgment that eating disorders are real medical illnesses brings hope to families who already know that their problems won't just go away. The grown Corbett women, for example, all still struggle with body image and health problems related to their eating disorders. Their mother, Margery, was hospitalized recently for dehydration from drinking too much alcohol and not eating enough. Liz sometimes freezes at the thought of going out to parties because she can't figure out what to wear. Cathie, who has a 3-year-old daughter and a 9-month-old son, purged during her second pregnancy and has damaged the enamel surface of her teeth from years of bulimia. Meanwhile, Bonnie continues to struggle with anorexia, 17 years after it began. She takes vitamins and mineral supplements to avoid anemia. She takes birth control pills to keep her hormone levels up. And she has recently started taking medicine to treat end-stage osteoporosis. At 35, she has the bones of an 86-year-old woman and says her hips would probably shatter if she fell. The whole family takes things one day at a time. "You get the cards you're dealt," says younger brother Rick, 31, the only sibling spared by the illness. Instead of cancer or heart disease, he says, his family got eating disorders. "Everyone has their own battles to fight," Bonnie adds. "This is ours."

SOCIETY'S UNHEALTHY OBSESSION WITH THINNESS

Leonard Stern

The idealization of thinness can lead to the development of disordered eating patterns, Leonard Stern observes in the following selection. Most experts agree that the media's emphasis on thinness has a significant impact on how women perceive their bodies, Stern writes. When those individuals who are already susceptible to eating problems are exposed to unrealistic cultural expectations about how their bodies should look, they are likely to develop a full-blown eating disorder, Stern reports. He also notes that the glorification of thinness in women is a recent development in industrialized societies; in earlier times, thinness was seen as a sign of illness or starvation, whereas heavier women were considered healthy and strong. Working to change societal attitudes about the ideal body and focusing on building self-esteem in children may help to prevent eating disorders in the future, Stern concludes. Stern writes for the *Ottawa Citizen*, a Canadian newspaper.

In 1873, the French physician Ernest Lasegue published an account of eight female patients who had developed a bizarre aversion to food and were starving themselves. This disease, however, existed before Lasegue came along. Richard Morton, an English doctor and preacher, wrote in 1689 of a girl with no appetite who resembled a "skeleton only clad with skin," yet who retained a compulsion to exercise right up until dying from her "consumption" (consumption being the catch-all label doctors invoked when something baffled them).

In the Middle Ages there were also reports of adolescent girls, "miracle fasters," who, claiming divine inspiration, stopped eating. In later centuries, people travelled far and wide to view oddities such as one Sarah Jacob, "the Welsh fasting girl," who starved herself to death in 1869.

Lasegue, though, was the first to study clinically what he called *"l'anorexie hysterique,"* or anorexia nervosa as it is known today. It was a strange malady, he marvelled. As his patients slowly starved themselves, skin turning yellow and faces hollow, their frantic parents imploring them to eat, the girls seemed puzzled at the fuss and calmly insisted, *"je ne souffre pas, donc je suis bien portante."*—I'm not suffering, I'm fine. Lasegue concluded that until sufferers recognized they were ill, treatment was hopeless.

Lucyna Neville, who co-founded Hopewell, an eating disorder support centre in Ottawa in 2000, recalls one time—there have been many—when she brought her daughter Michelle to the Children's Hospital of Eastern Ontario (CHEO). It was 1999, and Michelle, then 16, had been struggling with anorexia for several years. A CHEO psychiatrist had been seeing her, but that night there was no time to wait for an appointment and Neville took Michelle to the emergency room.

The family had just spent a long weekend on their sailboat, throughout which Michelle did not eat. In the first years of her daughter's illness, Neville begged and pleaded with her, just as the parents of Lasegue's patients had. Neville remembers awful scenes at the kitchen table: "I would cry, she would cry, we both cried." Girls with eating disorders typically don't feel good about themselves, and Neville learned that making Michelle cry only intensified the self-loathing. So on the boat, Neville held her tongue. "I'd say to her, 'Michelle, what will you have for breakfast?' She'd say, 'I'm not hungry, thank you.' This went on for three days. When we came off the boat, I said to my husband, 'I'm taking her straight to CHEO.'"

Michelle was emaciated, but the nurses, after taking her pulse and listening to her heart, felt she was not in mortal danger. Neville insisted they measure Michelle's vitals standing up. By then Neville had become a self-taught expert on the disease and she explained to the nurses that it's hard to tell how sick anorexics are when they're lying down. When Michelle got to her feet, her heart rate accelerated by 70 beats a minute and she swayed like a reed in the wind. Neville remembers hearing one nurse say "Oh, my God" before sliding an intravenous tube into Michelle's arm. Another tube, a force feeder, went into Michelle's nose and down into her stomach. All the while Michelle, bewildered at the commotion, repeated, "I feel fine."

A Medical Mystery

Eating disorders are medical puzzles. Diagnosis, treatment, prevention—experts can't reach consensus on any of these. It's hard even to say what constitutes an "eating disorder." So-called binge eating, for example, is often classified as a distinct disorder. Does this mean you have a disease if you go berserk at the buffet table? Is binge eating a function of how much you eat, or is the defining criterion loss of control? How many times does it have to happen? Or consider bulimia nervosa, characterized by binging and purging, that is, eating huge amounts and then deliberately vomiting or eliminating the food with laxatives. What constitutes a binge—a tub of Haagen-Dazs in one hour or in one afternoon?—and how often must you purge?

These classification difficulties, as scientists call them, make it hard to estimate the prevalence of eating disorders. It was once believed that only one of every 100 women developed anorexia. But to be considered anorexic, the patient was required to demonstrate amenorrhea (the disruption of her menstrual period and a sign of malnourishment). Many doctors today feel that the amenorrhea criterion should be optional, and that a diagnosis can be made based only on extreme weight loss, a debilitating fear of gaining weight and a disturbed perception of one's body size—in which case the occurrence of anorexia doubles to nearly two per cent of the female population. Bulimia nervosa, meanwhile, afflicts anywhere from two to nearly four per cent of girls and women.

"So what's the take-home message? About five per cent of young adult females will at some point develop a serious eating disorder," said Dr. Allan Kaplan, who heads the Program for Eating Disorders at the Toronto General Hospital. Dr. Kaplan became interested in the phenomenon during his medical residency 20 years ago and since then has become a principal figure in the Toronto Group, as he and his colleagues are known throughout the world of eating disorder research.

Medical stars, perhaps a reflection of their own competence, are often upbeat when asked what the future holds for the treatment of multiple sclerosis or Parkinson's or whatever their specialty happens to be. Not Dr. Kaplan. "Anorexia nervosa remains, for most patients who fall ill, a treatment-resistant, chronic illness with significant morbidity and mortality," he wrote in the April 2002 issue of the *Canadian Journal of Psychiatry*. "Over the past 50 years, little progress has been made in developing new effective treatments for the disorder."

Unusual Diseases

In 1978, the late Hilde Bruch, a 74-year-old professor of psychiatry at Baylor University in Texas, published a book summarizing her experience treating victims of anorexia. A medical pioneer, Bruch began studying eating disorders before the Second World War. It says something about the weirdness of these diseases that, after 40 years in the field, Bruch never lost her morbid amazement that they inspired.

Bruch recounted the defiant 14-year-old who told her, "Of course I had breakfast; I ate my Cheerio;" the 22-year-old who wouldn't lick stamps because she was terrified of possible calories; the walking skeleton who, with "iron determination," pursued her goal of thinness not only by restricting food but by swimming laps five hours every day. Although anorexics insist they aren't hungry, Bruch found that that's not true. The problem is not lack of appetite but a deathly fear of getting fat.

One clue that anorexics suffer hunger like normal people is that their behaviour mirrors that of people whose starvation is involuntary. Anorexics linger over food, drawing out the meal, as people do during times of famine. Prisoners of war had elaborate strategies to make one slice of bread last an hour. They are preoccupied with food, just as anorexic girls, Bruch discovered, "will not talk about anything else, becom(ing) excessively interested in cooking, often taking over the kitchen."

Bruch reported one patient, a 15-year-old girl, who would begin baking cakes and cookies after school and would go to bed only after other family members—not her—had finished the last bite. People who starve become creative in the way they prepare food, using whatever spice and flavouring is available, as though to create an illusion that the meagre offering is more bountiful than it really is. Psychiatrists observe similar habits in anorexics. It is a warning sign when a teenage girl begins mixing vinegar in her drinks or lavishing mustard on lettuce salad.

Recognizing Eating Disorders

Despite the early work of Bruch and a few others, eating disorders were not included in the *Diagnostic and Statistical Manual*, the official catalogue of mental illnesses, until 1980. The Canadian medical community has been at the forefront of the field—Toronto's Dr. Kaplan is president of the international Academy of Eating Disorders—but even in Canada eating disorders seem to have been neglected. The Ottawa Hospital did not establish a treatment clinic until 1997 (and now does a volume of some 200 new patients a year). CHEO finally created an eating disorders program in 2000. The delay is odd, considering that of major psychiatric diseases, eating disorders have one of the highest rates of suicide attempts and hospitalization.

Because recognition of these disorders came late, it will likely be a long time before they are fully understood. The best doctors can do is adopt a risk-factor model, the kind applied to other diseases whose etiology—whose cause—is uncertain. "It's hard to say one thing causes cancer, but a whole bunch of things put you at risk," said Dr. Kaplan. "If your mother had breast cancer, your risk of breast cancer is higher. Smoking increases the risk of lung cancer, and if you are genetically predisposed it may tip the balance. It's the same thing with anorexia, including the genetics." (He recently co-authored a paper that implicates a specific gene in the disease.) "Being put in a competitive ballet class at the age of five is going to increase the risk. Families can magnify the risk. Don't make weight and shape a focus in the family."

Malignant tumours usually don't show themselves until long after the organism has ingested the carcinogen. Similarly, says Kaplan, although eating disorders appear in adolescence, "The seeds for these problems are laid early in life."

A Media Connection?

There is consensus that the cult of thinness in the entertainment and fashion industry is linked to eating disorders in the general population. Experts disagree, however, on the significance of the connection. Some argue that the media celebration of unattainable bodies like those of Kate Moss or Britney Spears is almost entirely to blame. The feminist critic Naomi Wolf, in her book *The Beauty Myth*, advanced what seemed a conspiracy theory—that the thin ideal is a way to keep women distracted and powerless, weakened by the never-ending battle with their shape.

One problem with theories that blame Kate Moss and Britney Spears is that, if correct, anorexia and bulimia would be epidemic, which is not quite the case. Images of thinness are everywhere, yet the majority of adolescents do not develop full-blown eating disorders, though many do feel lousy about their bodies. It may be that exposure to magazine covers and music videos is a necessary condition, but not a sufficient one, for onset of disease. A hundred people can spend a weekend at a casino, but few will become compulsive gamblers. Access to alcohol will lead some drinkers toward alcoholism but not others. Existing predispositions are required. Clinicians are increasingly borrowing from addiction models in the effort to untangle the mechanisms of disordered eating.

Still, the glorification of thinness has been dramatic. One researcher took the time to chart the Miss Americas and Playboy playmates between 1960–80 and found that over the years they gained in height but dropped markedly in weight. The truth is, thin women do better. Studies show that slim women enjoy more upward mobility, in part because they attract men who have economic and social status. While thin women marry up, heavy women marry down. Little girls absorb this harsh reality. Eighty per cent of North American girls begin to diet by the age of 13. Childhood dieting and weight concerns are implicated in later development of eating disorders. In a study of British schoolgirls, 20 per cent of the dieters progressed to eating disorders, compared to three per cent of the non-dieters.

The Idealization of Thinness

It is not clear why industrialized societies, where eating disorders are most common, have come to idealize thinness. There was a time, not so long ago, when fat was desirable. Monarchs, as a show of prestige, carried their bulk with pride. It was a sign of power and prosperity that they could maintain large bellies. Still today, in the undeveloped world, where food shortages threaten, it is a status symbol in some countries to be heavy. But there are no food shortages in the West; instead, obesity is rampant. Thinness has become a sign of discipline and achievement.

Anorexia and bulimia have traditionally been diseases of the middle and upper class. Two British psychiatrists recently reviewed the cases of hundreds of anorexia patients and found that, based on the father's occupation, nearly 70 per cent came from "social classes one and two" (class five being the lowest). Research on this side of the Atlantic has found that African-American women, who are on average poorer and less educated, have fewer weight concerns and a healthier body image than white women, even though black women tend to be heavier. There is anecdotal evidence that this is changing, however. Women of all hue and background are showing up at clinic doors. "Cultural beliefs that traditionally have protected ethnic groups against eating disorders may be eroding as adolescents acculturate to mainstream American culture," wrote Toronto Group psychiatrists Paul Garfinkel and Barbara Dorian in 2001. The aerobicized bodies on MuchMusic and MTV are as often black as white.

The idealization of thinness "doesn't make sense," said Caroline Davis, a psychology professor at York University in Toronto. "From an evolutionary perspective, we should find heavier people more attractive. They are the ones more likely to survive because they lay down fat more easily, and our genetic forbears lived in times of shortage and famine." It was by way of an interest in sports psychology that Davis came to eating disorders. Competitive female athletes, she had discovered, are at risk for the disease. And it is also true, as Ernest Lasegue observed more than a century ago, that anorexics become more physically active as their weight drops. Davis dug out a graph plotting the weight loss and exercise pattern of one current patient. At the last weigh-in, the girl was 78 pounds, the lowest in six months. The intensity of her workouts was also the greatest it had ever been.

Intuition says that exercise is a conscious strategy to accelerate weight loss, but Davis believes it may be more complicated than that. If you restrict a rat's diet, the rodent, oddly, responds by using the running wheel. The less the rodents eat the more they run, and the more they run the less they eat, until they die. The rats are not thinking about losing weight. In humans, too, the deadly cycle takes on a life of its own, disconnected from the patient's original desires or volition. "I had one patient who said it was like a train that speeded up and that she couldn't stop," said Davis.

Studying Eating Disorder Victims

Davis is an experimental psychologist—a scientist, not a therapist. She doesn't treat women who come through her laboratory; she studies them. It's heartwrenching. "When I first started this work more than a decade ago, I remember saying to a colleague, 'I don't know if I'm cut out for this,' because I found it very distressing. It's an incredibly unglamorous disorder, and you see these children who seem to be blessed, often very bright and accomplished, and this thing gets a hold of them. I was seeing patients the same age as my two daughters, and it was devastating." (Her daughters, ages 31 and 27, have never had eating problems.)

Not long ago, Davis posted notices across the York campus seeking female volunteers for a study. One hundred young women were selected and given extensive questionnaires measuring how they felt about their appearance. One of the questionnaires, the Eating Disorder Inventory, is used as a screening instrument to identify women who are at risk for developing an eating disorder.

Each volunteer was told that a second, unrelated experiment was being conducted, for which the laboratory wanted to take their photographs. Actually, it was part of the same experiment. The women weren't told beforehand that they would have their photos taken because Davis wanted to catch them as they ordinarily looked, not dolled up. Afterward, Davis and her team had the photographs rated on a scale of attractiveness (eight judges, four women and four men, between the ages of 23 and 31, rated the Polaroids on a scale of 0 to 10, to the nearest 0.5.). The team then matched the photographs with the questionnaires. What they found was that the attractive women were those most preoccupied by their weight. Physical beauty, Davis discovered, is a risk factor for disturbed eating.

Davis theorized that because attractive girls and women enjoy social advantages, they learn to objectify their bodies—to measure their self-worth by how they look. This leads them toward dieting, which, for the unlucky ones, will metastasize into an eating disorder.

This hypothesis—that viewing oneself as a physical object can trigger disordered eating—explains why it is usually women and not men who succumb to the illness. Women are valued for their appearance, men by their wealth and status. It also may explain why the few men who do develop eating disorders are, according to anecdotal reports, often homosexual. Men, gay or straight, focus largely on looks when appraising potential mates. Gay men therefore objectify each other the way other men objectify women.

It came as no surprise that a medical team at Yale University recently discovered that gay men report the same degree of body dissatisfaction as straight women, and that the intensity of a gay man's dissatisfaction increases the more closely he is involved with the gay community.

Once an eating disorder has you, it won't let go. In 2001, two doctors at a New York state hospital reported the case of a well-groomed 92-year-old woman. She was 5-foot-9-inches and 98 pounds. She obsessed about food, was terrified of getting fat and gorged on prunes as a laxative to keep her stomach in the "correct shape." She ran laps around the hospital ward. Doctors could not determine exactly how long she had been anorexic, but guessed many decades. She was not depressed, psychotic or senile. Initially, she was seeking treatment for pneumonia. Only after she was admitted did an alert dietitian call in the psychiatrists.

Learning How to Get an Eating Disorder

Pilot programs in the prevention of eating disorders appeared more than 10 years ago. They worked this way: Health educators and gym teachers went into high schools and delivered detailed lessons about anorexia and bulimia. Students were spared nothing. They learned how vomiting four times a day rots the teeth; how laxative abuse wrecks the bowels; how starvation disrupts menstruation and causes a layer of downy hair to cover the body. Women who already suffered from an eating disorder were sometimes invited to speak to the class, much as pictures of wrecked cars are used to scare teenagers off drunk driving.

The programs were failures. The girls became knowledgeable about eating disorders, but this knowledge had no effect on their behaviour. Worse, to the horror of their teachers, evidence mounted that the lessons triggered eating disorders. Follow-up studies showed that giving girls information about eating disorders somehow normalized the condition. Students began practising the weight loss techniques—laxatives, vomiting—they had heard about. By the mid-1990s, panicky doctors were issuing calls to abandon these "information-giving" programs.

Even group therapy is dangerous, because when girls with eating disorders get together a twisted collusion can occur. Tips and secrets are traded: Tell people that you're a vegan to get out of meals; hide food in your napkin; never faint in front of your parents. During the time Michelle Neville was hospitalized and tube fed at CHEO, she learned from other girls on the ward to pump her own stomach and surreptitiously dump the contents. She only needed a syringe, which the girls secretly stockpiled. "The nurses had to start accounting for every syringe," says her mother Lucyna.

An Internet Community of Sufferers

The impulse to aid and abet each another is in full view on the Internet. Dozens of "pro-anorexia" Web sites have appeared since 2000. At first, health professionals thought the sites were hoaxes or grotesque jokes, set up to make light of eating disorders. One site, for example, offers the "10 Commandments of Anorexia," among which are: "Thou shall not eat without feeling guilty" and "Being thin is more important than being healthy."

These sites are not jokes. For some young women the disease becomes part of their core identity, through which they find membership in a larger community of fellow travellers. They don't want to be cured any more than converts to a religious order want to be saved from their "affliction." (Though as each girl strives to be the thinnest, it is hard to tell if anorexics are colluding or competing. Some theorists speculate that perfectionist and competitive personalities are risk factors for eating disorders.)

Allan Kaplan and his Toronto colleague Paul Garfinkel recently wrote that "more than any other psychiatric disorder, patients (with eating disorders) evoke intense feelings of hostility, anger, hopeless-ness and stress in therapists." Although researchers compare eating disorders to substance abuse and other addictions, there is a differ-ence. People with eating disorders, as Drs. Kaplan and Garfinkel wrote, "take pride in mastering their bodies (and) see the illness as an extraordinary accomplishment." Substance abusers, on the other hand, may deny they have a problem, but will agree in principle that drug abuse is bad.

Eating disorders are hard to treat because the patient is unwilling to abandon what she considers to be virtuous behaviour. Drs. Kaplan and Garfinkel have concluded that, sometimes, the therapist's most important role may be to provide comfort and empathy, similar to the approach "one would have for any dying patient."

Carla Rice also talks gloomily of an "eating disorder subculture" whose members don't want to get better. "There's been a few clients who I've worked with for whom the counselling has not been success-ful," she said. "They determine by the end of the counselling they don't want to relinquish their eating disorder. When we get there, there's nothing more I can do. I have to respect it. I don't like it but I have to respect it."

Eating Disorders as a Cultural Phenomenon

In the mid-1990s, the Regional Women's Health Centre of Toronto hired Rice to design a clinical program for women who were unhappy with their appearance. The Body Image Project, as it came to be known, is now a permanent addition to the Health Centre. Rice, who is 39, has a master's degree in education and is writing a PhD thesis at York University's department of women's studies. The Body Image Project, where she works as a therapist, has a distinctly feminist atmos-phere. Language matters here. You don't "treat" clients; you "counsel" them. Eating disorders are not illnesses but "struggles." Rice herself had disordered eating in her youth—she wouldn't say which disorder, or how severe—but today is almost grateful for it because it "propelled me into something that was really positive." The disease sparked a political awakening, a recognition of the challenges facing women.

Psychiatrists often "pathologize" eating disorders, complained Rice—they see anorexia and bulimia as mainly medical conditions. But Rice and other feminist therapists prefer to see them more as political or cultural phenomena, manifestations of injustice against women. In truth, most psychiatrists do recognize that eating disorders are a function of cultural and social pressures to be thin. Yet Rice feels that even the "more progressive" psychiatrists still feel that "it is only vulnerable women who develop problems. So there's a separation between all the normal women and then the women who develop weight struggles, and I don't see it that way. I always saw it as more of a continuum."

(To which Allan Kaplan replied, impatiently, "Eating disorders don't occur on a continuum. Most young women may not like their body shape, but it doesn't have a major impact on their physical or psychological well-being. For people with eating disorders, it destroys their lives. You wouldn't say that because 89 per cent of the population at any one time is coughing, they all have pneumonia.")

Changing Cultural Attitudes

One understands why feminists—though not necessarily Rice herself—might be tempted to blur these distinctions. If the aim is to purge society of oppressive images of female beauty, better to argue that all women are damaged by these images rather than just the five per cent who develop clinical eating disorders.

According to this approach, eating disorders are symptoms of social or cultural illness. It is not women who are diseased but their environments. And at the Body Image Project, Rice counsels women to fix their environments, what she calls their "social locations." The first step might be simply to remove mirrors and scales from the house and to stop watching television shows with skinny starlets. Rice said: "We have two options as women. One is to change our bodies to fit whatever social locations we find ourselves in, and the other is to change our social locations to fit our bodies." If a woman has friends who obsess about dieting, for instance, she should find new friends.

Prevention programs failed, it could be argued, because they assumed the problem of disordered eating resided in the heads of young women rather than in the world around them. It was useless to lecture teenagers about the folly and danger of dieting when, at the same time, they were bombarded by cultural messages telling them they can never be too thin. Thus feminists have begun proposing "ecological" prevention. A grandiose concept, it implies nothing less than the transformation of society, a transformation realized through mass education about the iniquity and danger of negative body image. The campaign begins with parents and teachers, then with school boards and communities. Once society begins to reject unrealistic images of female beauty, the popular media will follow. Cultural tastes are hard to move, but once dislodged, momentum sets in.

At least that's the theory. Skeptics will note that it will be a long, long time before men begin pursuing size 16 women as they do size 2 women. (To which feminists reply that transforming social attitudes has long been a feature in other health prevention programs, such as smoking and drunk driving.)

Focusing on Self-Esteem

But there may be a middle way toward preventing eating disorders, one that does not require a utopian paradigm shift. In 2000, a pair of Australian researchers—both women—conducted a study involving nearly 500 children aged 11 to 14 (most of whom, but not all, were girls). The children were randomly divided into two groups. One group participated in a nine-week program—one lesson per week— designed to develop their self-esteem; the other did not. The nine lessons, which included stress management and interpersonal skills, taught the children that they are unique individuals, that they are important and that each has an inherent self-worth.

Neither group knew that the project was an inquiry into disordered eating and body image. Even the teacher who taught the lessons was not told. At the end of the nine weeks, the researchers administered the Eating Disorders Inventory questionnaires to both groups of children. Those who had participated in the lessons showed a higher degree of body image satisfaction than did the control group. Of particular interest were the findings for girls who, before the study, had been identified as high risk for eating problems. The nine-week intervention significantly lowered their scores on the Drive For Thinness segments of the questionnaire.

Unlike the earlier, disastrous experiments where children were lectured on nutrition and received graphic information about disordered eating, the Australian exercise avoided issues of food or eating and focused only on self-esteem. To the extent it suggests that simply nurturing a child's confidence provides some measure of protection, the study is good news to parents. Building a child's self-esteem is common-sense parenting, requiring no specialized expertise.

Or so one hopes. "You'd be surprised," sighed Allan Kaplan. "Some parents don't know how to tell their kid that they are unconditionally accepted. Some parents and teachers tie the sense of acceptance to what their children look like or what they do." Kaplan added one other thing about prevention. "You want to start early. If you go in when they're 15 years old, it's too late."

THE PROBLEM OF NUTRITIONAL MISINFORMATION

Karolyn Schuster

Karolyn Schuster, a writer for *Food Management* magazine, examines the ways in which misunderstandings about nutritional information have contributed to the national obsession with thinness. Experts initially thought that the rise of consumer interest in health and nutrition would result in healthier lifestyles, Schuster explains, but instead many people are using nutritional information—and misinformation—in their attempts to conform to the thinness ideal. Kids are dieting at ever-younger ages, she points out, while adults are increasingly turning to fad diets and unregulated diet supplements. Most people do not know how to develop and maintain healthy eating habits, the author warns, and this lack of information can lead to eating disorders. Schuster suggests that adopting healthier body ideals and educating the public about the dangers of dieting may help solve the problem.

The scene is commonplace enough: a group of females earnestly discussing their ideal body weight and shape, the various parts of their bodies that fall short of that ideal, the diet/exercise plans they have tried in the past, and the weight loss programs they plan to try next. It is the composition of the discussion group that is startling: girls eight and nine years of age.

At a time when society sees them as giggling and care-free children, these girls are becoming tangled in concerns for their appearance and their weight that will, for many, develop into a lifelong obsession.

"The preoccupation with appearance has worked its way down in age so that we now have girls dieting in third and fourth grades," says Mary Orear, a veteran teacher who founded and directs Mainely Girls, a statewide advocacy and education organization in Maine whose goal is to increase opportunities for girls.

"The stigma of being fat overrides everything else. Ask them. These girls will tell you that it is worse to be in third grade and fat than to be in a wheelchair. We find a tremendous amount of self-loathing in middle and high school. You hear girls talking about their

Karolyn Schuster, "The Dark Side of Nutrition," *Food Management*, vol. 34, June 1999, p. 35. Copyright © 1999 by Penton Media, Inc. Reproduced by permission.

own body parts like they're pieces of chicken."

Nutrition experts and healthcare providers were not prepared for this. They expected, as did most of the rest of society, that the heightened national interest in nutrition and health topics we have seen in the '90s would translate into a healthier, more active population.

But ongoing research and recent statistics say that is not the case, that, in fact, all this talk about nutrition has a dark side. The dark truth is that first, consumers are sometimes misusing the legitimate information on nutrition and health that is being disseminated; second, misinformation on these subjects is often disseminated as freely as accurate information; third, misleading nutritional claims are being made by manufacturers and marketers alike; and fourth, on the larger societal scale, a new body frame ideal has been adopted along the lines of "never-too-thin."

The result is a national obsession—an unhealthy, self-defeating, depressing obsession—with losing weight.

Too Young to Diet

"America's children are afraid to eat," writes Frances M. Berg, M.S., L.N., a well-known nutritionist and author. "Instead of growing up with secure and healthy attitudes about their bodies, eating and themselves, many kids fear food and fear being fat. It's a national public health crisis.

"Weight issues have become an obsessive concern for American children of all ages," continues Berg. "Clearly it is a national crisis when harmful attempts at dieting are common in the third grade and even earlier. It is a crisis when more than two-thirds of high school girls are dieting and half are undernourished.

"One in five take diet pills, and many girls as well as boys are using laxatives, diuretics, fasting and vomiting in desperate attempts to slice their bodies as slim as they can. This is the point to which our weight-obsessed culture has brought us."

Karin Kratina, M.A., R.D., formerly a nutrition therapist and now a consultant with The Renfrew Center, which specializes in the treatment of eating disorders among women, says treatment of the disease is "becoming more complicated because society is reinforcing eating disorders.

"Thin is not just in; thin is imperative. Everyone has a set point of weight at which exercise and a healthy diet come into balance and the set point is different for everyone. It's the yo-yoing of weight gain and weight loss that people are putting themselves through that is dangerous."

The Damage Being Done

The national weight obsession is one component of the current crisis. Another is the prevalence of misinformation, half-truths and out-of-context data that feeds this obsession. The third component is internet technology, which has made information of any type, regardless of its accuracy, value or even morality, instantly accessible to anyone with a computer, regardless of age, suggestibility or maturity.

The dark side of nutrition is that efforts undertaken in the name of becoming healthier are, in fact, damaging our physical, mental and emotional well-being. Consider the following trends:

• An increase in the incidence of eating disorders, primarily anorexia and bulimia, among adults, adolescents and children. Evidence: Solid, national statistical evidence is limited, primarily because of the lengths to which people go to hide eating disorders as well as the lack of any public health initiative in this area.

However, the National Eating Disorders Organization estimates that one in 10 teenagers and college students suffers from eating disorders, more than 90% of them female. The National Institute of Mental Health estimates that instances of anorexia and bulimia have doubled in the past 10 years, with the sharpest increases among females aged 15 to 24.

• Increased participation in fad diets, often promoted in bestselling diet books. In her book, *Afraid to Eat*, Berg estimates that dieting—in all its forms—is big business, with a price tag of $30 to $50 billion annually in the U.S. alone. That intimidating dollar volume increases the difficulty of regulating or policing the diet market.

• The proliferation of products that claim to aid in weight loss, including prescription drugs, over-the-counter diet pills, laxatives, diuretics, herbal and vitamin supplements, gums, sprays, and even cigarettes, very often used by teenage girls to reduce their appetite for food. A 1993 study of television commercials for diet products found that such promotions comprised about five percent of television advertising. One doesn't need statistical proof that the percentage has increased. A review of newspaper and magazine headlines on any newsstand substantiates the popularity of diet-related news, advice and case studies

Relying on Supplements

"Herbals are the latest bandwagon," says Michele Cavoto, R.D., FADA, nutritionist for James Madison University's dining services, in Harrisonburg, Virginia.

"I'm seeing a lot of gingko, green tea, blue green algae," she says. "I discourage students from using herbs. I tell them they're not regulated, that the concentrations aren't consistent, that we have no way of knowing what concentrations and what volume of any particular herb is helpful and—perhaps more important—at what concentration and volume they are harmful.

"With students, I stress the idea of getting the nutrients they need from the food they eat—without relying on herbals or even vitamin supplements. There's so much we don't know about how the body processes supplements."

Claudia Plaisted, assistant professor of nutrition at the University of North Carolina, also supports the nutritional message of relying on food for the nutrients you need.

"There are chemical properties of food that we are only beginning to understand," says Plaisted. "There are more than 10,000 phyto-chemicals out there in the foods we eat that contribute to our physical health. We don't know enough about those chemicals to package them in pills yet. In addition, some of the herbals we're seeing right now contain drug-like compounds and can have side effects."

• Narrowed focus used by consumers in designing their diets. The prime example is the preoccupation with fat to the exclusion of everything else. "Everyone says, 'eat less fat,' Less than what? Most consumers don't know what the starting point is," says The Renfrew Center's Kratina.

• Adoption of ideal body weight standards that are much thinner than in past years, fueled primarily by the fashion and film industries. Naomi Wolf, author of *The Beauty Myth*, argues that the accepted ideal female body type is now at the thinnest five percent of a normal weight distribution, leaving 95% of females above that ideal.

Misinterpreting the Information

"We're seeing an epidemic of misinformation. I can't believe the extent to which students are relying on all sorts of misinformation in making their food selections," says Penny McConnell, MS, RD, director of nutrition services for Fairfax County Schools, Fairfax, Virginia.

"I teach a Kids Cooking course to fourth graders in our district and I am horrified at the number of them who are not drinking milk because they have decided that milk is fattening. This is happening at the same time that we are seeing very serious health effects from calcium deficiencies in our older population."

"There is less nutrition education being taught at some grade levels because it's being crowded out by new health subjects, like conflict resolution and healthy relationships," says Shannon Stember, R.D., nutrition education coordinator for Portland Public Schools, Portland, Oregon. "The increased emphasis on higher standards for math, language arts and science also is reducing the time spent on health."

Stember says that what kids ask about in her classroom parallels what the media and their parents are focused on and that the most common question she is asked is "Is this a good or a bad food?"

"Students and teachers want to rank foods as positive or negative, put them in a 'don't eat' or 'do eat' column," says Stember. "I ask them to consider the quantity of the food eaten (portion sizes) and the frequency (how often) with which the food is eaten before making a judgment about its effect on their health.

"The fact is you can provide nutrition information but you can't be sure how people will interpret it and whether they will take it to the extreme. It's also true that individuals have different nutritional needs. Some kids are eating too many empty calories but others are not getting enough food."

"Nutrition can be like a religion for people," says Kristy Obbink, Portland's assistant director of nutrition services. "If they've got it in their minds that something will work for them, it's very difficult to change their minds."

Nutritional Pitfalls in College

Nutrition misinformation is no less of a problem at the college level. At Boston University's dining services, an Aramark account, campus dietitian Royletta Romain says that college students try it all—food jags (one-food diets where they eat nothing but grapefruit, for example), diets extremely low in fat (which rarely produces desired weight loss because sugar calories replace the fat calories), and fad diets in which weight comes off quickly but also returns quickly.

Barbara Boden, Aramark's marketing director at Boston University, says promotions during National Nutrition Month recognized the fat concerns of students but also tried to encourage the consumption of a wider variety of foods, especially fruits and vegetables. Among the items offered: sweet potato and spinach soup, baked stuffed tofu and banana crisp.

Romain says, "My recommendation always is that students start by educating themselves on both the Food Pyramid and serving sizes and then use that knowledge to design lifelong, sensible approaches to eating. Serving sizes are key. A one-ounce slice of bread is one serving but students often eat a giant five-ounce bagel and count it as one bread serving."

"The type of poor student eating behaviors is going to differ by campus," says Dianne Davis, R.D., a part-time nutrition consultant to both the dining services and athletic departments of Vanderbilt University. "A private school such as Vanderbilt that has high academic standards and pulls students from a high socio-economic background is going to have a student population that is very concerned with their appearance. That sets you up for different nutrition problems than a school that pulls a different student body.

"The problem here is a lack of knowledge about how to eat right," she says. "Many students don't like vegetables, they hardly ever eat fruit. Some of them have never had a nutrition course. They just don't choose foods wisely. They are unable to interpret and evaluate information and relate it to the basic needs of their bodies."

Davis, who would like to see nutrition a mandatory course for Vanderbilt's undergraduates, says, "My personal opinion is that putting nutrition information on the serving line is not the way to combat poor eating habits because the students can't put that information in context. There's a fat phobia out there so when you tell them an entree has 10 grams of fat, they say 'I'm not eating that.'

"What we should be telling them is: This is why you need fat in your diet; this is how your body uses fat; this is how much fat you should consume daily; this same entree also contains the following important nutrients that your body needs."

Davis says this lack of basic understanding of nutrition leads to bad decisions on food consumption.

"The way they diet is to eliminate certain food groups from their diets, or eliminate all fat, or not eat anything for a day. Athletes decide they can eat all the carbohydrates they want, so they load up on bagels, rice, potatoes, frozen yogurt, but they don't touch anything green and they seldom eat fresh fruit. Non-athletes, too, who are avoiding fat also may overeat carbohydrates. Generally, though, I see more problems with not eating enough than with eating too much.

"As a society, we like quick and easy fixes," she says. "My message is boring—variety, balance, moderation—but I'm looking to develop healthy, lifelong eating habits. Students are looking at fitting into a dress for Saturday night's dance."

Fat's Fallout

The price society pays for its national obsession with weight is a staggering one on many fronts. More adults, adolescents and children are malnourished and more are obese than ever before. Based on National Institutes of Health definitions, more than one-half of all Americans age 20 to 74 are overweight and one-fifth fall into the "obese" category. The financial and emotional resources we devote to losing weight are massive yet our efforts are unsuccessful for the long-term because pounds shed by dieting almost always are regained when "normal" eating habits are resumed.

The biggest price may be paid by our children. They are adopting nutritional habits in their years of greatest growth and development that carry the potential for lifelong nutritional deficiencies affecting health, energy and activity.

James Madison University's Cavoto says, "We used to see students develop eating disorders in college. But we've been moving down one school year each year I've been working in the field. Eating disorders started in high school, if not middle school, for the students I am seeing now."

"Eating disorders are an alternative language, a language these girls learn when English doesn't work," says Monika Woolsey, M.S., R.D., who has designed a self-esteem curriculum for teenagers that revolves around teaching them to communicate, cope with problems and resolve conflicts.

"If we can teach them to express themselves and get their needs met through normal communication channels, it is my conviction that they won't need to hide behind eating disorders," says Woolsey.

"Dietitians are partly to blame," says Woolsey. "We burned our bridges by being overzealous in the past on subjects like fat and cholesterol. We shouldn't have been focusing on fat; we should have been teaching them how to question the media messages on nutrition and how to separate out the advertisements for junk food.

"We've got kids passing out in class because they haven't eaten, or their hair's falling out, or their nails are breaking. We've got them so afraid of fat that they don't eat anything," she says. "For too long, we focused on foods that are 'bad' for you. We took so many foods away that there's nothing left for them to eat."

Curing the Obsession

Healthy eating advocates argue that the cure for our current crisis lies in the national adoption of more realistic weight ideals that accommodate a wider range of sizes, a greater tolerance and acceptance of larger bodies—in ourselves and in society, and a nutritional message that preaches variety, balance and moderation.

A move is under way among many registered dietitians to adopt a no-diet approach to their work with patients, organizations and the public. A number of dietitians interviewed for this report admitted that their efforts to ban diets within the American Dietetic Association (ADA) is nothing short of a revolution, a revolution centered in the ADA practice group known as SCAN, for Sports Cardiovascular and Wellness Nutritionists.

"The reliance on meal plans and diets is keeping dietitians from being recognized as the nation's nutrition experts," says Linda Omichinski, founder and president of HUGS International, a center for information and resources that promotes a lifestyle without diets. "Our emphasis on diets has kept us from positioning ourselves as the leaders in the health of the public. Dietitians are starting to speak out on the idea of health at any size. That is our message for the future."

"I don't do diets," says Cavoto, who counsels James Madison University students with nutritional problems. "That starts the cycle. I promote the idea that healthy eating is based on balance, variety and moderation. Am I hungry? Am I satisfied? Eat when hungry, stop when satisfied."

"Dieting behavior causes eating disorders," says The Renfrew Center's Kratina. "Dieting is a restrictive cycle in which you learn to ignore your own body's hunger. Dieting teaches you to follow someone else's eating plan and not trust your own body and the signals it sends. Eventually you become totally confused by those signals. If your body is signalling that you're hungry, you're not sure you really are hungry. If you accept that you are, in fact, hungry, then you're not sure what to eat. In treating eating disorders, we help patients get in touch with these internal signals and learn how to respond to them."

Plaisted, of the University of North Carolina, who has worked with eating disorder patients for 13 years, says, "What we have been doing as professionals and what we have been saying as a profession has moved the public toward eating disorders. Diets don't work—period. The results are dismal. I don't hold the diet industry alone accountable. All of us who work in this industry are accountable. We've got to learn to teach people to make peace with food, teach them what normalized eating is. The relationship with food and eating should be a healthy, wonderful, delicious part of your life. We've got to find some food balance, some life balance.

"It may be a great idea to offer low-fat items on your dessert menu," continues Plaisted. "But you don't want a dessert menu that's all low-fat items. That sends the message that fat is bad. Our message should be that bodies come in all shapes and sizes. We should be looking for the healthy long-term in which we encourage a real, normal pleasure with food."

Breaking the Diet Cycle

Omichinski says her opposition to diets evolved from her personal disillusion with the dieting background in which she had been trained.

"I was setting people up for failure," she says. "They would work with me for awhile and they would lose weight. But they would go off the diet and the weight would come back. Their attitude always was, 'The diet worked, I failed.' It got so former patients would avoid me in the grocery store because they didn't want me to see them with the weight back on."

The school curriculum Omichinski developed for pre-teens and teens under the HUGS logo evolved from an anti-diet program for adults she had created. The school program is designed to keep the diet cycle from advancing so teenage dieters do not become adult dieters.

"Our non-diet approach promotes health at any size," says Omichinski. "We teach teens to reconnect with their bodies. The diet method is a punishment for the way you look. It provides you with an excuse to put blame on yourself.

"Face it—only 10% of the population is going to be skinny. If a teen is genetically meant to have a lower body weight, our approach to eating and activity will move them in that direction. But if they aren't, we'll help them accept that also.

"Part of it, of course, is self-esteem and assertiveness training," she says, "There's so much fat prejudice out there. The larger teen needs to learn to say I'm active. I'm eating no differently than you eat. This is the size I am meant to be."

EATING DISORDER WEBSITES: A DISTURBING TREND

Nancy J. White

In the selection that follows, *Toronto Star* reporter Nancy J. White explores the proliferation of pro–eating disorder websites on the Internet. White explains that these sites, which are run by people who have eating disorders, offer tips and support to others with their condition. However, the author reveals, this support is not aimed toward recovery; instead, the website participants encourage each other to continue and improve upon their disordered eating behaviors. She points out that health care professionals are alarmed at this development, in which anorexia and bulimia are portrayed as positive lifestyle choices rather than illnesses. While someone who is not already vulnerable to eating disorders is not likely to get one from visiting these sites, White observes, those who are already suffering from eating disorders can be aversely affected, deciding to forgo treatment or experiencing setbacks in recovery.

Alone at night, she enters her secret cyberworld, surfing the sites with the photos of sliver-thin women, their collarbones and ribs protruding under their skin.

She joins the chat rooms where women hungrily exchange tips on losing yet more weight and fooling family and friends into thinking they're eating. She posts messages and reads what others have to say, often pouring out their shame for not being perfect—for eating.

"It's so nice to have a place where people understand what you're going through, where they have the same messed-up emotions," says Julie, a 19-year-old university student who didn't want her real name used.

Web sites supporting eating disorders evolved in the late 1990s, often from personal diaries that anorexics and bulimics posted online.

"You can say what you want, like taking the filter off your mouth and letting it all spill out," Julie says. "I've gotten to know people on the sites. As an anorexic, you don't have a lot of friends."

Nancy J. White, "Anorexics Caught in the Web," *Toronto Star*, February 22, 2003. Copyright © 2003 by Toronto Star Newspapers, Ltd. Reproduced by permission.

But her nightly forays are filled with guilt. "It must be like what people visiting pornography sites feel," says the young woman from the U.S., who has been hospitalized twice for anorexia and is now in therapy.

Do the Web site visits keep Julie in the disease?

"I don't know," she says quietly.

A Dangerous New Trend

Medical experts hold no such doubts.

"They're incredibly dangerous," says Dr. Allan Kaplan, who holds the Loretta Anne Rogers chair in eating disorders at Toronto General Hospital. "They legitimize a potentially deadly disorder as a lifestyle choice. I am appalled by them. I can't use strong enough language."

Anorexia nervosa—extreme restriction of food, leading to significant weight loss—is the most deadly psychiatric illness for young adults. The mortality rate ranges from 10 to 15 per cent. Bulimia nervosa—regular binge eating with compensating purging or exercising—affects an estimated 3 to 5 per cent of the population, with young females particularly at risk.

Some cyberspace meeting places proclaim themselves "proud to be anorexic." Some tout anorexia and bulimia as lifestyle choices, not diseases, and refer to them as "ana" and "mia," their best friends.

"It's like saying cancer is good and here's how to get it," says Christopher Athas, vice-president of the National Association of Anorexia Nervosa and Associated Disorders (ANAD) in the United States.

In 2001, the sites were banned from several Internet servers, including Yahoo's. But the pro-ana and pro-mia pages popped up elsewhere. "It's like an underground subculture," says Julie. Some sites even promote the wearing of a special red bracelet as a show of solidarity among like-minded anorexics.

The number of sites is hard to gauge. Although they're plentiful and easy to find, sites may appear or disappear overnight. Some record thousands of hits, but a lot certainly come from repeat visitors. Many offer links to other pro-eating disorder addresses, or to a newer genre of "pro-acceptance" sites. The latter don't promote the disease, but don't preach against it, either.

Many parents and health professionals want the pro-eating disorder sites prohibited. The U.S. group ANAD scans the Net regularly and keeps after Internet firms to expunge them from servers.

But a ban is hard to accomplish on the freewheeling Web, and some worry the women would go further underground, rebels with a cause.

"The individuals who run and visit the sites aren't bad people," says Karin Davis, program co-ordinator with the National Eating Disorder Information Centre. "They're sick and struggling."

Their voices are varied, and from all over the world.

A Web of Obsession

A 45-year-old divorced mother from Australia logs on when her three children are asleep. An anorexic in her 20s, she began restricting food again when her marriage fell apart. "I couldn't control its disintegration, but I could control my eating," she told the *Star*. From the Web sites, she has learned ways to cover up her scanty eating so her children don't notice.

Some messages sound desperate, filled with self-loathing. "To all you who think this is some thin plan, f— you. . . . This is about trying to deal with yourself who you hate," says one woman in a chat room.

Some are simply naive. "I want to become ana," posts a 12-year-old.

Many seek encouragement, ways to become better anorexics. "I feel like a terrible failure," writes a woman who barely ate all day, then devoured a night-time snack. "I'm still proud of you," commiserates another woman. "Hold your pretty lil' head high and have a better day today."

Victoria, a 24-year-old Toronto college student who didn't want her name used, stumbled on the sites two months ago by accident and now spends four hours a day roaming them, always when her roommate is away.

"It drives me nuts if a friend is thinner than me," says the woman, who has been obsessed about her weight since she was 17. "Friends say I look fine, but what do they know? I get paranoid. I think they're humouring me, so they can be thinner."

On the Web sites, she likes the pictures of dangerously thin supermodels, she says, but not the ones of severe anorexics. "Those make me sick. They're not sexy."

Victoria insists she's not one of those "death-wishers." She just wants to lose weight. She eats less than 500 calories a day. (The recommended intake for a young woman to maintain healthy weight is 1,800 to 2,200 calories a day.) She has a goal weight of 116 pounds.

Will she be able to stop? "I think I can," she says, after a pause. "The thought of being too thin is gross. I want to be perfect."

At New Realities Eating Disorders Recovery Centre in Toronto, psychotherapist Orit Morse hears this all the time. But then people reach their goal and still feel fat. "It progresses to less and less," Morse says. "It gets distorted."

The Web sites, she says, only affirm their denial, their belief that they're not sick.

Manipulating the Vulnerable

Experts note that the sites aren't likely to create an eating disorder unless certain vulnerabilities are present. Those include a genetic predisposition, personality traits of perfectionism and compulsivity, and serious underlying emotional problems, such as lack of self-esteem or fear of emerging sexuality. A big risk factor is being a woman. The female brain chemistry is more sensitive to dietary manipulation, says Kaplan.

But for the vulnerable, the sites can provide a dangerous endorsement. Some even post warning signs: Do not enter if you don't already have an eating disorder or if you're considering recovery.

"I've had a girl, free from binging, purging or restricting food for four years, go on the sites in a bad moment, and the recovery unravelled," says Morse, founder of the New Realities centre. "One or two statements hook them."

Or they become competitive. One 18-year-old patient would get revved up when she found someone on a site who was lighter than she was. "She'd think, 'I'll show her I can be a better anorexic than she is,'" explains Mississauga psychotherapist Terri Marques. The patient was surfing five hours a day, neglecting school and friends.

Some anorexics and bulimics recognize that their Internet interludes jeopardize recovery.

"Every friend you make through it adds to your identity as someone with an eating disorder—that if you recover, you'll be nothing," a 17-year-old Toronto high school student, an occasional pro-ana site visitor, told the *Star*.

But others dismiss the idea that these Web pages keep them sick. Even if the sites disappeared, they say, our culture is full of restricting or purging triggers, from photos in magazines to seemingly innocent comments.

Sarah from Tennessee insists she'd be ill regardless.

"If I were put in a box with no windows and no personal contact and no mirrors, I would still have my eating disorder," she told the *Star*. "The sites help me feel less like a disease and more like a person."

Their popularity has not only sparked grave concern in the eating disorders field, but has also raised questions. "Is there a need for a sense of community and support that we're not offering?" asks Davis.

Creating Supportive Websites

In February 2003, Sheena's Place, a Toronto eating disorders support centre, launched an online magazine, *Flushed*, about dealing with anorexia and bulimia. It is created by the clients and appears on the centre's Web site, and will soon have a message board.

"There's nothing how-to about it," says Ann Kerr, program director at Sheena's Place. "It's more about 'I've been there, this is what it feels like.' It's a more positive use of the Internet."

The Net actually offers a range of choices, including anti-pro-anorexia sites as well as recovery ones. But some anorexics and bulimics say the recovery pages tend to be too preachy and don't allow them to be honest about their feelings.

"You might be on a recovery chat room, but you're still puking into a bucket next to your computer," says one former bulimic.

Most sufferers feel extremely ambivalent about recovery, about shedding their eating disorder personality.

"I'm in a conundrum," says Julie. "I don't like what the eating disorder has done to my life. But it's such a big part of me, I don't know who I am without it."

That's how Shannon Bonnette felt when she started surfing the pro sites. But after a while, the over-all sadness and sameness of the postings got to her.

"There would be a moment of excitement—someone would lose five pounds," Bonnette says.

"But soon she'd gain again and write about hating herself. It was the same pained messages over and over. I realized I wanted to change."

Recovered now for three years, she runs a Web site of her own, what she calls "a safe zone," with no lecturing or bashing. "It's about acceptance and education," says Bonnette, 25, a college psychology student in the United States.

Others have also started pro-acceptance sites. "It's a huge shift in the last couple of years," says Bonnette.

One Web site offers the viewer either anorexia pages or recovery pages, stating that it is no longer "pro-eating disorder," but now "pro-choice."

Explains the home page: "The creator is currently attempting to change her way of life."

ETHNIC MINORITIES AND EATING DISORDERS

Susan McClelland

According to *Maclean's* associate editor Susan McClelland, for many years eating disorders occurred primarily among white women. People in non-Western countries did not idealize thinness in women, McClelland states, and ethnic minorities living in Western nations were unlikely to value thinness as highly as their white counterparts. But the Western world's obsession with body image is starting to have global influence, she explains: Anorexia and bulimia are showing up for the first time in places like South Africa and Fiji. Western television shows are partly to blame, McClelland reports; for instance, a study revealed that after only a few years of exposure to these shows, women in Fiji began using laxatives and vomiting to lose weight. In addition, the author points out, ethnic minorities in the United States and Canada face growing societal pressure to be thin, with a correspondent increase in the incidence of eating disorders.

When Zahra Dhanani was just seven years old, her four-foot frame already packed 100 lb.—so her mother, Shahbanu, put her on her first diet. "My mother, a fat woman, daughter of another fat woman, thought if I was skinny, different from her, I would be happy," says Dhanani. The diet, and many after, did not have the desired effect. By 13, Dhanani was sporadically swallowing appetite suppressants; at 17, she vomited and used laxatives to try to keep her weight under control. There were times when she wanted to die. "I had so much self-hate," recalls the 26-year-old Toronto immigration lawyer, "I couldn't look in the mirror without feeling revulsion."

The hate reflected more than just weight. "It was race," says Dhanani, who had moved with her family to Canada from East Africa when she was 4. "I was straightening my hair—doing anything to look white." Her recovery only began when, at age 19, she started to identify with women in other cultures. "I came to realize that there were people who revered large women of colour," says Dhanani, who now says she loves all of her 200 lb. She blames part of her earlier eating disorders on the images in western media: "When you have no role models to counteract the messages that fat is repulsive, it's hard to realize that you are a lovable human being."

The Western Body Ideal

Body image may be one of the western world's ugliest exports. Thanks to television, magazines, movies and the Internet, rail-thin girls and steroid-built beef-boys are being shoved in the faces of people all over the world. As a result, experts say, cultures that used to regard bulk as a sign of wealth and success are now succumbing to a narrow western standard of beauty. And that, in turn, is leading to incidences of eating disorders in regions where anorexia and bulimia had never been seen before. But body-image anxiety in ethnic cultures runs much deeper than weight. In South Africa, almost six years after the end of apartheid, black women still use harmful skin-bleaching creams in the belief that whiter is prettier. "We're seeing a homogenization and globalization of beauty ideals," says Niva Piran, a clinical psychologist at the University of Toronto. "It's white. It's thin. And the result is that people come to identify less with their own cultures and more with an image in the media."

In most cultures, bigger was considered better until the 19th century. "The larger a man's wife, the more he was seen as a good provider," says Joan Jacobs Brumberg, a professor of American women's history at Cornell University and author of *Fasting Girls: The History of Anorexia Nervosa*. That began to change during the Industrial Revolution, she says, as women in the United States and Great Britain began to see thinness as a way to differentiate themselves from the lower classes. By the 1920s, fat was seen as unhealthy. And in the burgeoning magazine, movie and fashion industries, the women depicted as being successful in love, career and finances were slim and almost always white.

The Increase in Body Obsession

Still, eating disorders are not a modern affliction. Records of women starving themselves (anorexia) date back to the medieval period (1200 to 1500). As Brumberg notes in *Fasting Girls*, during this time, a woman who did not eat was admired for having found some other form of sustenance than food, like prayer. Yet, until the twentieth century, the number of women who fasted was low. But, particularly over the past 30 years, the number of anorexics and women who self-induce vomiting (bulimia) or use laxatives has increased dramatically. "It's generally this obsession with the body, constant weight-watching, that introduces a person to these behaviours," says Merryl Bear of the Toronto-based National Eating Disorder Information Centre. It was commonly believed, however, that sufferers came predominantly from white, middle- and upper-class backgrounds. Experts thought ethnic minorities were immune because of their strong ties to communities that emphasize family and kinship over looks alone.

Studies done in the United States with Hispanic, black and Asian college students, however, show that women who are alienated from their minority cultures and integrated into mainstream society are prone to the same pressures of dieting as their white counterparts. In a recent study of South-Asian girls in Peel, Ont., 31 per cent responded that they were not comfortable with their body shape and size. Fifty-eight per cent compared their appearance with others, including fashion models—and 40 per cent wanted to look like them.

Television's Influence

Some of the most compelling research comes from Harvard Medical School psychiatrist Anne Becker, who was in Fiji in 1995 when the government announced that TV, including western programs, would be introduced. "Fijians revere a body that is sturdy, tall and large—features that show that the body is strong, hardworking and healthy," says Becker. "Thinness and sudden weight loss was seen as some kind of social loss or neglect."

In 1998, Becker returned to Fiji and found that this had all changed. Her studies showed that 29 per cent of the girls now had symptoms of eating disorders. Many said they vomited to lose weight. But what was most alarming were the girls' responses about the role of television in their lives. "More than 80 per cent said that watching TV affected the way they felt about their bodies," Becker says. "They said things such as, 'I watched the women on TV, they have jobs. I want to be like them, so I am working on my weight now.' These teenagers are getting the sense that as Fiji moves into the global economy, they had better find some way to make wages and they are desperate to find role models. The West to them means success and they are altering their bodies to compete."

Cheryl McConney has felt the pressures to alter her body, too. The black 32-year-old native of Richmond Hill, Ont., co-hosts a daytime talk show on cable TV. And although it has not been difficult for her to get where she is in her career, she is concerned about how to navigate her next step. "Looking at Canadian television, I don't see many people who look like me on air," she says. At five-foot-five, and weighing about 145 lb., McConney has never been told she should lose weight. Still, in 1998, she went on a six-month, high-protein, low-carbohydrate diet, hoping to look better in front of the camera. She shed 20 lb. "I felt good. People in the studio thought I looked great, but it wasn't easy to maintain." Within a year, she had gained it all back.

The Issue of Race

For McConney, race has been more of an issue. An industry insider jokingly told her that she would do better if she dyed her hair blond.

And recently, she was discouraged from applying for another on-air host position because of what the casting agents said they were looking for. "They wanted the 'girl next door' and 'peaches-and-cream' pretty, not chocolate and cream," says McConney, adding: "It was pretty clear some women were not invited to participate because of their skin colour." As to the girl next door part: "I said it just depends where you live."

While McConney says she is determined to make it on air despite the barriers, Linda, who requested *Maclean's* not use her real name, may not be around to see her success. The 19-year-old—part South African and part East Indian—has anorexia. She says trying to fit into a Canadian suburban community played, a big role in her illness. "I was never proud of my different religion, different skin colour," she says. "I would put white baby powder on my cheeks just to make me look white." What alarms her now, Linda says, is that with her skin pale from malnutrition and her weight fluctuating between 75 and 85 lb., other young women often come up to her and say, "You look so good, I wish I looked like you." But she adds: "What they don't know is that my body is decaying. People glamorize eating disorders. But what it is is a lifetime of hospitalization and therapy." As long as the western media promote thinness and whiteness as the pinnacle of beauty, stories like Linda's will remain all too familiar.

CHAPTER 3

LIFE WITH AN EATING DISORDER

WHEN FOOD IS THE ENEMY: THREE GIRLS' STORIES

Teen Magazine

Three girls recount their struggles with anorexia and bulimia in the following article from *Teen Magazine*. Brooke Casey and Denise Gray (not their real names) tell their stories to writer Stephanie Booth, while Elonne Stockton relates her experiences in her own words. Each girl describes how she developed her eating disorder. Brooke became anorexic because she thought she could only feel good about herself if she was thin. A chubby child, Elonne developed anorexia in response to cruel taunts from other kids. Denise's bulimia began after her mother encouraged her to lose weight, saying that boys would not like her if she was fat. Brooke and Elonne detail their experiences with therapy and hospitalization and their hopes for full recovery. Denise, however, admits that she has yet to tell her parents about her bulimia, even though she knows that she has a serious problem and has been unable to stop bingeing and purging on her own.

Eating disorders (EDs) run the gamut from mild to serious, and treatments vary. In some rare cases, girls get better simply with the love, support and understanding of their families; other cases require hospitalization. In most instances, some professional intervention, such as counseling by a specialist in the field, is necessary. Ahead are three girls' true stories of their struggles with an ED.

Brooke's Story

Before I became anorexic, people complimented me on how thin I was—not how pretty I was or how great I dressed. By high school, I thought being thin was my only positive physical attribute. It felt good knowing that I may not be as cute as the cheerleaders, but I was skinnier. I started worrying that if I ever gained weight I'd become ugly.

That's why I stopped eating all fast food and anything with more than 2 grams of fat—basically, anything I liked. The worse something tasted to me, the safer I felt eating it. I'd usually have herbal tea for breakfast, a plain salad and diet soda for lunch and a cup of white rice for dinner. I ate slowly, trying to make every bite last. So many foods were "bad" to me. The hot fudge sundaes and fried cheese I once loved came to gross me out. When I felt hungry, I'd take a bath or go to bed early. Drinking a lot of hot water filled me up. I gave myself strict rules: no eating after 6 p.m., no eating more than half of anything and each time I walked into my kitchen—even for just a glass of water—I'd have to "pay" for it with 50 sit-ups.

I was in constant motion three hours a day to burn calories. I'd bike-ride, do exercise tapes or swim a mile at the YMCA (sometimes I'd walk the two miles there and back). Exhaustion made me forget how hungry I was.

In six months I went from 122 to 87 pounds—which felt more like 870 pounds to me. My jeans were hanging off of my 5-foot 6-inch frame, but I thought I looked huge. I was constantly freezing, even with long underwear and two pairs of wool socks on. Everyone would be wearing shorts while my fingers and toes would be turning blue.

My life was counting calories, weighing myself and standing nude in front of the mirror while I hunted for fat. I didn't have much energy. My grades dropped, and if it was a choice between exercise and going out with friends, I would sweat through two aerobics classes. Friends said, "You need to fatten up," but I thought they were jealous—I even thought my mom was. I'd get so mad when she asked, "Are you eating?" What was she trying to do—make me fat?

When I fainted in aerobics, everyone realized how bad I'd gotten. My body was so undernourished, I had to go to the hospital.

When I got there, the nurses asked me about my diet habits, and I totally lied. I know they must have been freaked out at the sight of me. My face was hollow and pointy, and my shoulder bones stuck out. The doctors took lots of blood and hooked me up to an IV to get some nutrients into my body. I stayed in the hospital overnight, and when I was released the next morning, the doctors gave me the name of an eating disorders specialist. Although I tried to deny the problem, it was obvious to them what was going on. They warned me that if I didn't change my habits, my life could be in danger.

The Road to Recovery

I'm sure going to a counselor saved my life. I promised my mom I'd go just once, without any intention of ever going back, but I liked Carol.

From the start, Carol explained that EDs have a lot to do with how you feel about yourself. When I feel fat, what I'm really feeling is failure. I learned I was a total perfectionist. It was pathetic realizing how much I hated myself—I went through half a box of tissues that first visit.

Carol made me keep a log of what I ate. She taught me not to see food as "good" or "bad." It was a struggle. Wherever I went, I worried I would lose control and eat everything in sight. I even wondered if just smelling food caused weight gain. For months I didn't go to the movies because I'd have to smell popcorn. It was a huge triumph when I ate my first chicken sandwich in a year. I could only eat a third of it, and I felt I had to walk around the block afterward, but Carol said it was a baby step.

It's been two years since I was in the hospital, and I see Carol once a week. I'm on antidepressants, and my weight's up to 104. I'm trying to like myself more, but it's tough. "You're so skinny, it makes me sick," this girl at the mall said. I felt like responding, "You're right. It makes me sick too."

Elonne's Story

I've had trouble dealing with my weight since I was 12 years old. Eighth grade was the worst. I was going through a chubby phase, and kids were really cruel. To gain control, I basically stopped eating. Not all at once, of course. First I started cutting down on fat. Then meat. Then I wouldn't touch any fat or food that I enjoyed. My parents pleaded with me to eat, but losing weight became an addiction. I knew the calorie and fat counts of everything. I would never eat in restaurants because I didn't trust them. I was afraid that I would become that chubby child again if I ate regular meals. I mostly ate alone. I was such a picky eater, it was embarrassing sitting there with friends. In time, I managed to push away most of my friends. Now I realize they must have been scared of me. Who wants to hang out with a walking corpse?

As I continued to give up food, I ultimately had to give up the one thing that made me feel good: running. In tenth grade I started on the track team and went for 8-mile runs every morning. After my runs, I'd eat a slice of diet bread, a quarter of an apple and a scoop of soy protein powder. For the rest of the day I'd snack on fruits, vegetables and low-calorie crackers. I never allowed myself more than 900 calories a day. By the time I was in twelfth grade, my body didn't have enough energy to run. I had to quit.

In school I was always a good student, always on the dean's list, but it was never good enough. I was really hard on myself. When I got less than an A, I felt horrible, and I would eat even less—making it harder to concentrate and memorize or learn anything.

During stressful times I ate the least. The only thing I could control was food. I weighed my lowest, 89 pounds, in the summer of 1998. I was transferring to a new college, my sister moved away and my parents were having problems. This time, however, I didn't go back to eating my normal amount. I seriously restricted my calories, until the time I thought my heart stopped beating.

Reaching for Help

It happened when I transferred to Columbia University in New York. I was 19 years old, 5 feet 7 inches and 94 pounds—and my body was exhausted. On the first night in my dorm room I knew I was in trouble. I couldn't sleep, I felt faint and I could barely breathe. I didn't feel my heart thumping. It was the longest night of my life. I was scared but didn't tell anyone because no one would understand. My fear of eating was killing me: My body wanted me to eat or die. In the morning, I went to the campus health center. An employee there rushed me to the hospital.

I expected to be in the hospital for a couple of nights, but it turned out to be a month. My organs were failing. They shut down when they didn't receive the food they needed to function. I had to drop out of school, and I was moved to a hospital in Connecticut to be closer to my family. Without their support, I wouldn't be here. The doctors and nurses in the hospital made me eat—they would hold my hand while I ate. I couldn't do it alone.

I still can't completely do it alone. I was released from the hospital weighing 100 pounds. It's been two months, and I'm continuing therapy, going to weekly weigh-ins and taking medication to help me eat. I'm even able to eat cake sometimes. I'm proud to be up to 120 pounds, and when I look in the mirror and say, "Elonne, you look fat," I can say, "Stop it. You're not fat." I'll be recovering from anorexia forever, and every morning I thank God I'm alive. It takes a lot of hard work to get better, but I know I'm on my way.

Denise's Story

The first time I threw up, I was 8 years old. I'd just seen a talk show on TV where all these women confessed they purged to keep their weight down. They'd eat as much as they wanted, then stick their fingers down their throats. I remember thinking, "I could do that." I was chubby and always trying to be as thin as my mom. She wanted me to be thin too—she put me on any diet she read about in magazines. "Boys would like you more if you weren't so fat," she said once when I complained about eating nothing but grapefruit all day. I didn't even like boys yet. When I was 10, my mom gave up bothering me about my weight. But I guess I was already brainwashed.

Now, every time I eat something, even an apple, I feel guilty, like I've let my mom down. She doesn't have to say anything; a little voice inside me screams, "How can you eat so much, you fat pig! You're so gross!" That's when I puke everything up. My life revolves around food—what I eat and when I throw up. We have four bathrooms at home, so it's easy to hide. I'm 5 feet 5 inches and have weighed anywhere from 90 to 150 pounds, but my parents still haven't caught on. At first, I mostly threw up dinner, but then I discovered bingeing.

From Bad to Worse

Now, if I'm feeling really bad about myself, usually if I had a crappy day or a fight with my parents, I sneak food into my room. Food fills me up and makes me feel better, but only for a few minutes. Then the misery hits. I'll go through a sack of candy corn, a loaf of bread and a bag of chips, and I drink lots of soda—it makes it easier to throw up. Waking up in the middle of the night to binge is like waking up on Christmas morning. It's sick, but that's how excited I get.

After I binge, I feel woozy and light-headed—almost like getting laughing gas at the dentist. I feel almost happy. Then this guilt rises up inside me, and I have to stick my finger down my throat. I start crying when I'm puking. I worry I won't be able to get all the food back out. I keep gagging until I get the dry heaves. A couple of times, I jammed my finger down my throat so hard I scratched myself and tasted blood. I've spent so many hours with my head in the toilet, it doesn't disgust me anymore.

All day long I bite my nails, thinking about when I can be alone so I can binge. Weekends are the worst, since my parents are home more often.

I'm not stupid. I know about bulimia. I know that stomach acid has worn the enamel off my teeth and that I'm putting stress on my heart. Being bulimic is like being a smoker: You know it's not good for you, but you can't stop. I know I should talk to my parents, but I'm worried they'll be more disappointed in me. I've found some help on the Internet. There are a lot of girls like me, and we pour our hearts out to each other. Some of them don't think they're sick—they even trade puking tips. That's so sad. I wouldn't wish what I do or how I feel on anyone.

MY MOTHER GAVE ME ANOREXIA

"Juliette Potter," as told to Stacy Colino

In the following selection, Juliette Potter (not her real name) describes how her mother's obsession with her weight led Juliette to develop anorexia. Juliette explains that her mother, who herself suffers from disordered eating behaviors, began to limit Juliette's food intake when she was only four years old. As Juliette gained the weight that was normal for a growing child, her worried mother would organize contests to see which one of them could lose the most pounds. By the time Juliette was a junior in high school, she had developed full-blown anorexia. Juliette states that, with therapy and hospitalization, she has started normalizing her relationship with food. However, Juliette confides, she has found that she must keep her distance from her mother because of her unhealthy influence. Stacy Colino has written for *Cosmopolitan, Parents,* and *Working Mother.*

For as long as I can remember, my mother focused on my weight. I was never heavy as a kid, but I had a big appetite and a little bit of a belly, and that worried her intensely. By the time I was 4, my mom had already replaced my apple juice with Diet Coke, and I continued to diet throughout my childhood. Whenever I lost weight, she would get really excited and literally dance around. Later on, I realized that my mother's way of thinking was twisted, but by then, it was too late: I had developed a deadly eating disorder.

A Mother's Influence

I grew up as an only child in a somewhat unsettled household. My parents divorced when I was 9, and I went back and forth between their homes every week. My mother and I were more like friends than mother and daughter, but she was still a big influence on me—and her own eating habits were very unhealthy. Her favorite diet was one where she wouldn't eat all day, then for one hour at night, she could eat whatever she wanted as long as it was within that hour. As she struggled with her own cravings, my mom tried to limit my food intake as well. If we went out for a pizza and I reached for a second slice, she'd say, "Don't you think you've had enough?" I was a growing kid, and when my pajamas would get too small, she'd warn me that I had to eat less.

Soon, I figured out my own ways to curb my appetite. In fifth grade, I bought diet pills at the drugstore and took them for about a month. Sometimes, when I wanted to lose weight, I would go for a week eating nothing but bagels. As I got older, I started developing different food rules—for example, I could have pizza after school only on the days that I also had gymnastics because then I could work off the calories. My mom and I would go grocery shopping together, and we'd stock up on low-fat foods like pretzels, tuna, and frozen yogurt. There was no letup, not even on our vacations to Club Med, where my mom would orchestrate a contest of who could lose the most weight while we were there.

During the summer of 1997, I turned 16 and spent a month taking an SAT prep course at the University of California in Los Angeles (UCLA). By that point, my eating habits had become very strange—I'd concoct weird combinations like pickles and ketchup or sandwiches with just sprouts and honey mustard and while I was there, I lost about 10 pounds. When I flew home and got off the plane, the first thing my mom said was "Oh, my God! You look great!" Then she took me shopping for a whole new wardrobe. I had begun my steep descent into anorexia.

Spiraling Out of Control

By the fall of my junior year, I was counting calories more and eating much less. I'd have coffee or tea in the morning and I wouldn't eat all day, but I'd drink lots of water. Then, at eight o'clock at night, I'd have frozen spinach, cooked in the microwave, with ketchup. I was eating 150 to 300 calories a day—my max was 500—and that was counting gum and hard candies. At a certain point, a switch went off in my brain, and I didn't have any control over what I was doing.

In three and a half months, I lost 20 pounds. My weight dropped down to 91 pounds—at 5 feet 5 inches and with my build, I should have weighed around 125. I was out of it and confused all the time. I also stopped getting my period. But I felt proud of how thin I was and was shocked at other people's negative reactions. One time, I wore overalls to school, and everyone acted really funny around me. Apparently, the pants were so baggy that I looked skeletal, but I just couldn't see it at the time.

Neither could my mother. My boyfriend called her several times, begging her to take me to a doctor. Finally, she took me to my pediatrician, who said "Sometimes, teenagers get sad" and told my mom I was fine. But after seeing me one weekend, my dad stepped in and made me go to a doctor who specializes in eating disorders. My mom came with me, and when the doctor told her I weighed 91 pounds, she started crying. It was as if she needed a concrete number to finally realize that something was really wrong with me.

Dealing with the Problem

The doctor said I needed to be hospitalized, so in December of 1997, I was pulled out of high school and spent a month in an adolescent-medicine unit on Long Island. It was basically a refeeding program, although there were also therapy sessions about body image. Every morning, I had to step on a scale. If I lost any weight, I'd have to wear a hospital gown all day. If I didn't finish a meal, I'd have to drink an Ensure, a meal-replacement drink. If I didn't do that, I'd get a feeding tube up my nose. I felt controlled and caged, but inevitably, I started gaining weight. After my hospital stay, I was in day treatment for another six weeks, so I didn't go back to school until February of 1998.

At the time, I still weighed only 100 pounds, but my eating habits had gotten better. The doctors stressed that it was important for me to have family meals, but during a family therapy session, my mother confessed that she did not feel like she could handle the pressure because she worked until eight at night. So I moved into my dad's home. For a while, I was doing okay, but then eating became stressful again—there were just too many choices—and I started backsliding and eating less. It wasn't long before my weight was back down to 88 pounds.

During the summer before my junior year, I was seeing a new doctor who warned me that unless I turned things around, I would have to go back to the hospital. I knew I needed to gain weight if I was going to make it to college, but after all those years of unhealthy eating, I didn't know how. That's when I started bingeing. Eating during the day was too stressful, so I'd fast all day, then eat 2,000 to 7,000 calories' worth of food at night—mostly cookies, waffles, cereal, and peanut butter—and go to sleep so I wouldn't have to think about it. Then I'd wake up and start all over again. Naturally, I started gaining weight—I put on about 40 pounds during the school year. Every two weeks or so, I'd see my mom, and she'd tell me I looked nice. Everyone around me was so excited that I was no longer stick-thin, but the bingeing made me feel out of control and horrible about myself. I managed to graduate from high school and go off to college, but I was stuck in a vicious cycle and couldn't stop.

Breaking the Cycle

So after two years of bingeing, I became anorexic again. Bouncing between the two extremes became my pattern. I had to be hospitalized two more times, most recently in Arizona in the spring of 2001. The doctors and therapists there were able to make me see how I had to change my way of thinking about food, and I finally reached a turning point. Since then, my treatment has been going well—I'm in therapy, and I also take medication for anxiety and depression. I still eat most of my calories at night—although I will drink a smoothie for lunch—but I'm working on overcoming that habit.

At the age of 20, my eating is very different than it ever has been: I no longer consider any food bad or completely off-limits. My weight has stabilized at 115, and I feel okay about that, even though my mom always told me that she weighed 110 in college and we're the same height. Recovering from an entrenched eating disorder can take a long time, but I'm at a point where I'm trying to stop judging my bad eating habits and start figuring out what else is troubling me.

At the moment, I don't have much of a relationship with my mother. I speak to her maybe once a month and see her even less frequently. For years, I tried to get her to look at some of her own issues with food, but she has resisted. I love her very much, and I think she's a wonderful person in many ways, but because she hasn't been a healthy influence, I feel that I need to keep my distance for now. My father and stepmother have been supportive, and someday, I hope my mother and I will be closer in a healthy way. In the meantime, I'm trying to find ways to nurture myself. I live with a friend in New York City and work full-time as a sales rep for a marketing company, plus I'm going to college part-time, so my life is really busy. I feel confident that I will be able to overcome my eating disorders. It'll just take some time.

MAKING WEIGHT: A MALE ATHLETE'S STRUGGLE WITH EATING DISORDERS

John DiConsiglio

In the following article, John DiConsiglio describes the experiences of Mike Rogerson, who first developed eating disorders as a teenage athlete. As DiConsiglio explains, Mike embarked on an intense workout plan in order to compete on his high school's wrestling team—and to please his demanding father, who was critical of his weight. Before long, Mike found himself caught in the bingeing and purging cycle of bulimia, the author reveals. Concerned about his health, Mike's friends and teachers urged him to get treatment, but Mike denied he had a problem, insisting that only girls get eating disorders. But when he began vomiting blood—a problem caused by the damage his bulimia had wreaked on his digestive system—Mike agreed to seek help. Unfortunately, DiConsiglio writes, Mike later developed anorexia, a condition he is still struggling to overcome. DiConsiglio is a contributor to numerous publications, including *Scholastic Choices, Science World, Redbook,* and *New York Times Upfront.*

For the life of him, Mike Rogerson couldn't figure out why he was being called down to the library in the middle of the school day. The 15-year-old high school sophomore from Davenport, Fla., was certain that he had no overdue books. What could be important enough to drag him out of class?

Mike was really astonished when he swung open the library doors. Seated around a table were his best friend, Tom Wilson, and three of his favorite teachers. At first, Mike thought he was in trouble—or that something had happened to his family. But his English teacher put a hand on Mike's shoulder and said, "Mike, something is going on with you. I think you have an eating disorder. And you're not leaving this library until you get help."

"Are you crazy!" Mike said. "Girls get eating disorders. Not guys." But Mike was dead wrong. In the space of a month, he'd lost more than 50 pounds from his 6-foot 5-inch frame—dropping from 214 pounds to 160. Like millions of young people, Mike was suffering from an eating disorder. And, like many others, Mike never imagined that diseases like anorexia and bulimia could strike a male.

It's true that most people with eating disorders are female, but males also suffer. According to one study, one in six eating-disorder victims are men or boys, totaling more than 1 million males in the U.S. Most, experts say, are athletes struggling to control their weight for competition.

"Eating disorders in men aren't well understood. And to an extent, they aren't taken very seriously," says Vivian Hanson Meehan, R.N., founder of the National Association of Anorexia Nervosa and Associated Disorders (ANAD).

"Many men deny they have an eating disorder," she says. "It's hard to get them to accept help."

Denying the Problem

That day in the library, Mike wasn't looking for help, though his friend and teachers knew he had a serious problem. He was exercising incessantly—running three miles a day with weighted garbage bags taped beneath sweatpants. He was throwing away his lunch every day.

"I insisted there was nothing wrong with me," says Mike, now 20. "I was just dropping a few pounds for wrestling. I told them I'd be over it in a week or two."

Sadly, Mike was wrong. He still hasn't beaten his eating disorder—though he has been under a psychotherapist's and medical doctor's care for more than five years. His weight has dropped to as low as 127 pounds, but when he looks in the mirror, he sees an obese monster. He had originally suffered from bulimia—where he binged on massive amounts of food and then "purged" by throwing up or using laxatives and diuretics. Now he is anorexic—he starves himself, fasting for as long as a month at a time.

His inability to eat has caused massive internal damage. A certain amount of everyone's body weight has to be fat. The kidneys, liver, and other organs need fat to function. Mike's eating disorder has left his kidneys and liver badly damaged. His bulimia has deprived his body of potassium, which can lead to heart failure—the prime cause of death related to eating disrders. Indeed, a lack of fat and potassium has caused Mike's heart to shrink.

Feeling Worthless

Mike thinks his problem began because of a bad relationship with his father. "He was verbally abusive toward me," he says. "He's a harsh guy. He was always calling me fat and lazy. He would tell me I'd never amount to much in life."

Mike was an A student, but felt worthless. To please his dad, he went out for the wrestling team. "I'm tall, so I weighed over 200 pounds," Mike says. "But all the other guys in my weight class were made of muscle. I knew I couldn't compete with them." Mike decided he had to drop enough weight to qualify for a lighter weight class.

He started an intense workout regime. But when he failed to lose enough weight, he turned to a different solution. He began binging and purging. He ate enormous quantities of food, downing hamburger after hamburger. Then, when he was alone, Mike forced himself to vomit.

"I thought it was just temporary, until I made the weight," Mike says. "But when I made the weight, I was so weak that I couldn't wrestle."

That's when his friends and teachers cornered Mike in the library. Then, a few days later, in the middle of history class, Mike began vomiting blood. It turns out that his constant forced vomiting had torn the lining of his stomach. His mom rushed him to a doctor, who delivered sobering news.

"He told me that what I was doing would eventually kill me," Mike says.

A Tough Road Back

Mike agreed to get help. Eating disorders are curable, and most cases are not as severe as Mike's. The most successful treatment, experts say, combines therapy to heal the psychological scars, and food reeducation to teach sufferers how to eat healthy again. Mike has had some victories, but each time he has fallen back into defeat. While he had his weight up to nearly 160, after a recent relapse he was back to 137.

The worst part, he says, is the loneliness. "No one understands this," he says. "Every day, from the moment I wake up to the time I go to bed, I think about this. This isn't a normal life."

But Mike hasn't given up hope. "Right now, I'm focusing on staying alive," he says. "And every day that I'm still here gives me another day to fight."

ON THE ROAD TO RECOVERY

Galina Espinoza, Mike Neill, and Sophfronia Scott

Reporters Galina Espinoza, Mike Neill, and Sophfronia Scott write for *People* magazine. In the following selection, they tell the stories of six individuals—five women and one man—who are recovering from anorexia. According to the authors, studies have shown that only 33 percent of anorexics make a full recovery. However, the authors assert that these six individuals may well beat the odds: With the help of therapy, nutritional counseling, and family support, they are working to maintain their health and to guard against possible relapses. The authors describe the various routes to recovery taken by each anorexic profiled in this account, as well as relating their hopes for the future.

In June 1995 Judy Tam Sargent, 33, a doctoral student in nursing at the University of Michigan at Ann Arbor, launched a Web site detailing her 14-year battle with anorexia nervosa. Soon she was receiving up to 40 e-mails a day. "A lot of people wrote to me, 'I'm struggling. What can I do to help myself?'" she recalls.

That question confounds not only the nation's 8 million anorexics—88 percent of them young women, many of whom are perfectionists or suffer from low self-esteem—but health care professionals as well. According to a 1999 Harvard study of 136 anorexics seeking treatment, such as hospitalization and psychiatric help, only 33 percent achieved full recovery (defined as maintaining 95 percent of optimum body weight, among other criteria, for eight weeks) within the 90 months they were followed. Moreover, 40 percent of those who had succeeded suffered a relapse within four years. "The chronic course of eating disorders . . . suggests the need to identify these problems early," the Harvard team wrote, "and to intervene before the disorders become intractable."

Despite these odds, people such as Jenny Lauren, and the five others featured on the following pages, are battling back—successfully—from their years-long bouts with anorexia. "It's a long, hard road," says Lauren, 29, who has been in recovery since 1997. But, she says, "I don't see food as the enemy anymore. Food helps me now. It's taken four years to feel like I'm finally coming up from the dead." Sargent agrees: "Some people ask, 'When did you wake up and have some magical revelation and were recovered?' Unfortunately it doesn't work that way. It's a gradual process." But one that to them is well worth the effort.

Back from the Brink

Standing atop a snow-covered hill in Amesbury, Mass., in January 2001, savoring the chilly winter air, Jennifer Shortis, 20, felt that she was on the edge of a revelation. With her at the Amesbury Sports Park was a group of 12 fellow patients from the eating-disorders program at Hampstead Hospital in Hampstead, N.H. They were there for a day of inner-tube sledding. The intended lesson: Exercise can be fun.

Shortis, however, also walked away with brand-new insight about the toll her anorexia had taken—and the progress she had made. "It's things like this that make me so grateful," she told program director Monica Ostroff. "I couldn't have had this experience before."

In fact, just six months earlier, Shortis was far from enjoying the pleasure of a winter day's play. Distraught over her inability to beat anorexia and the financial burden it was placing on her family, she was threatening suicide. Starting in 1996, the 5'3" Shortis had wasted away from 124 lbs. to 70. And despite repeated medical intervention, her condition was so intractable by the summer of 2000 that her parents' insurer—which had already paid more than $100,000 in anorexia-related costs—balked at paying for more treatment.

Terrified that her parents might have to mortgage their house in Baldwinville, Mass., Shortis told her family that she "was just going to end it all, that I wanted to die so this would all be over with."

But Shortis's mother, Marlene, 56, a teacher's aide, father, Thomas, 59, an engineer, and six older siblings refused to let her give up. They had her admitted to Hampstead and persuaded the insurance company to cover a roughly $18,000, one-month stay. Shortis believes the experience saved her life: "From the minute I walked in the door, everybody was so happy and so welcoming that I knew it was going to go right."

A Growing Compulsion

Until that point, Shortis felt as if little had gone her way. Shy and sensitive, she was frequently teased in school. "It could be about the kind of clothes I was wearing or some remark I'd made," she says. "It made me feel like something was really wrong with me." Then, in August 1996, she began training with her high school field-hockey team. Soon exercise became a compulsion. "I'd ride a three-mile loop on my bike three times a day, then go for a walk, then go for a run," says Shortis, and every day she would do at least 2,000 stomach crunches. "She thought if she lost weight, she'd have more friends," says her sister Carrie, 27, a physical-therapy aide.

At the same time, Shortis reduced her meals to little more than rice cakes, yogurt and fat-free turkey sandwiches. "I'd aim for 800 calories," she says, "and if I ate 801, that was too much." By October 1996 she had lost 20 lbs. Her concerned parents, on the advice of their pediatrician, took Jennifer to a psychologist. "She told us, 'This is a quick fix, a couple of visits,'" says Marlene. She was wrong: Shortis would spend 3½ years going from one treatment center to another. At one facility, she was treated alongside patients with severe psychiatric problems. In another, being watched 24 hours a day by a staff member proved so stressful, she says, "I wet the bed because I didn't want to go to the commode in front of somebody."

All the while, she continued to get thinner, until her suicide threat led to her stay at Hampstead. "Jennifer was very willing to do the work once she knew people believed in her," says Ostroff, who herself spent 10 years as an anorexic before recovering in 1994.

One of only 10 Hampstead inpatients, Shortis bonded with the staff. "They sat and watched you, but they ate with you too," she says. "The conversation at the table was normal." Shortis also flourished, she says, because the program atmosphere was positive, not punitive: "At other hospitals I'd hide food I didn't want."

After a month she was released on an outpatient basis. "I felt trusted," she says, "like they didn't look down on me as some kind of low-grade person with a problem." By May 2001 Shortis was deemed recovered, and now she speaks to other patients at Hampstead about her experience.

With her weight up to 95 lbs. (her target weight is 100), Shortis eats three meals a day and snacks in between—fuel that comes in handy now that she's a full-time student at Mount Wachusett Community College in Gardner, Mass., and a part-time aide for special-needs preschool students. "I even feel hungry," Shortis says, "which I didn't for a long time."

For her family, no words could be sweeter. "It was a hard road," says her mother, "but we're on the other side of it now. It's real nice to have our daughter back."

Born to a World of Fashion

Santa Fe is a long way from New York City, which is how Jenny Lauren, 29, the niece of fashion designer Ralph Lauren, likes it. Tucked behind the walls of her one-story adobe home, she paints and writes and continues to heal from an eating disorder that, four years ago, devastated her 5'4" body. "It's all about simplifying my life," she says. "My motto is live like a kid—the kid I stopped being early on."

As a child, Lauren was striking. With raven hair and mesmerizing blue eyes, she looked as though she had stepped out of one of the picture-perfect American-lifestyle ads for which her uncle is known. In fact, at age 7 she modeled for his company runway shows. "People would gape at her and say, 'My God, look at that beautiful child,'" says her father, Jerry, 67, Ralph's brother and head of the fashion dynasty's menswear division. "She didn't understand that attention and it upset her."

Then, at 10, Lauren entered a world where she was considered less than perfect. At summer dance camp in Lenox, Mass., she noticed that, while she was talented, her muscular frame did not measure up to the slim figures of her classmates. "I was looking in the mirror feeling this intense loneliness," Lauren says. "I thought right then that I was going to starve myself." In retrospect she believes she got the idea from the 1981 TV movie *The Best Little Girl in the World*, about anorexia. "I remember thinking, 'Wow, I could do that,'" she says. "It was about having control."

"I started getting letters from her," recalls her brother Greg, 31, a Los Angeles actor and painter. (Another brother, Brad, 34, is a film editor in Manhattan.) "They would say, 'I'm really nervous because the other girls are skinny, and I'm scared about how many calories are in toothpaste.'" Back at home Lauren continued to be plagued by thoughts of having an imperfect body. Her family's involvement in the fashion industry didn't help. "I got mixed messages," Lauren says. "They would say, 'We want you to be healthy,' then, in the same breath, 'Oh my God, you look so beautiful, so chiseled.'"

An Obsessive Cycle

By ninth grade Lauren was exercising obsessively, running six miles a day and doing calisthenics at night. That December she dropped to 85 lbs. "My lifestyle was so tiring," she says. "I went from being a popular, fun girl to just not caring." Soon after, she met a bulimic classmate who introduced her to Ipecac, the vomit-inducing medication usually intended to treat accidental poisonings. "I thought, 'Wow, I can eat all this chocolate and then just get rid of it,'" she says. Instead, dehydrated and weak after two days, "I got really sick. My dad found me lying on the bathroom floor," she says.

Still, Lauren continued using Ipecac, and in the winter of 1987 her family had the 11th grader hospitalized for four months. "I was so upset," says Lauren's mother, Susan, 59, a guide at New York City's Metropolitan Museum of Art. "You want to tell her, 'You can't do this, you're going to kill yourself.'"

With the counseling of her high school principal, Lauren's outlook improved enough for her to finish classes and enroll at Manhattan's Barnard College in 1990. But soon, again fearful of gaining weight, she slipped into old patterns. After graduating in 1995 with a degree in art history and fine arts, the then-105-lb. Lauren moved to Santa Fe, where the cycle continued. "I felt like I was doomed," she says.

Within eight months Lauren moved back to New York City and soon developed severe bloating and weakness in her lower abdomen.

By 1997 she could barely walk. It took doctors months to diagnose her with small-bowel enterocele, a condition in which the space between the rectum and the vagina stretches and the small intestine falls into the larger cavity. Doctors say the condition was likely caused by Lauren's bingeing and purging and the resulting strain on her digestive system.

Forced to Recover

Surgery and months of painful rehabilitation to learn to walk again ensued, which Lauren says forced her into recovery. "I was stripped of all my addictions," she says. But it wasn't until late 1997—when she met Dr. Richard Pico, a psychiatrist at New York City's Mt. Sinai Hospital—that Lauren rebounded. "He was the first to validate my physical pain," she says. "That helped me to start healing."

Lauren began seeing Pico three times a week, taking antidepressants and keeping a diary of her thoughts and activities, all of which helped her progress. Food, though, remained a challenge. "Everyone was telling me to eat normally, but I didn't know what that meant," she says. "I was living on laxatives and, at some points, chocolate sorbet and alcohol."

For years following the surgery, eating proved physically painful, but Lauren gradually pushed herself to consume easily digested foods like boiled chicken and scrambled eggs. By 1998 Lauren felt strong enough to move back to Santa Fe. She no longer takes medication but sees a therapist once a week. To ease the pain that remains in her pelvic muscles and back, she does gentle exercise, like Pilates and swimming, and has regular sessions with an osteopath.

Still working on accepting her size 8 body, Lauren no longer weighs herself. But she often wonders whether she would fall into old habits if she were to move back to New York City, which she finds too fast-paced and rife with images of thinness. "I'm not going to lie and say I look great and feel great," she says. "If I could be a size 6 and be comfortable, that would be the Jenny I'd like."

Losing Weight to Fit In

Flipping through a photo album, Toni Tahoun comes upon a picture. There she is, head-turningly slim and the height of 1970s chic in miniskirt and boots. By her side: her leisure-suited and sideburned boyfriend du jour. "This," she says wistfully, "was in the years when being a stewardess was still very glamorous."

And when airlines, including Trans World Airlines (TWA), for which she has worked for 30 years, insisted that female crew members maintain a fashionable image that had little to do with their actual job description. "In those days," says Tahoun, "they were very strict about weight. I was so scared about those weekly weigh-ins." Trying to make the grade—in her case, about 130 lbs. on her 5'5" frame—says Tahoun, started her long, downward spiral into anorexia. "My weight was the one thing I could control," says the now 57-year-old grandmother of two, "and my favorite diet was absolutely no food. Then I tried to eat only fruit for a long time. That screwed up my digestive tract. Sometimes I'd eat only a few vegetables a day. And I loved diet pills."

The daughter of truck driver Eddie Harvey and bookkeeper Nina, Toni was 3 when her father died—and 14 when she eloped with Army helicopter pilot Odis Henley. Divorced from Henley in 1969 (they have four sons), the Tacoma, Wash., native embarked on her dream job at age 28. "I got started flying late," she says, "so it meant a lot to me. I was going to do whatever it took." As she traveled the world, Tahoun became conscious of something else. "I was," she says, "a black woman in a white world, and I was always alone and insecure. I was dating rich men only and I had to make weight."

Sharing the Disorder

As anorexia and its common companion bulimia—chronic bingeing and purging—took hold, Tahoun began sharing weight-loss tips with her 13-year-old stepsister Nina. Even after Nina moved to West Germany with husband, Dennis Clinton, an Army sergeant, she continued to follow Tahoun's advice. When they returned to the United States in 1986, Tahoun could see that Nina had learned the lessons too well. "She was about 80 lbs. and 5'9"," says Tahoun. "I knew she was in trouble and I knew I was in trouble."

Married to Manhattan restaurateur Mohamed Tahoun in 1980, Toni weighed just 105 herself. She was diagnosed in 1981 with bulimia and anorexia, and not long afterward she even checked into an eating-disorder treatment center in San Juan Capistrano, Calif., for three months, telling her family and friends that she was going to a spa. Once out, though, she says, "I started all over again."

After her second marriage foundered in 1986, Tahoun, down to less than 90 lbs., sought help again—and this time she meant it. "I called the special health section of TWA," she says, "and they found me this great doctor I have to this day. I called my sister and told her that we would fight this thing together. I told her to hang on."

But Nina couldn't hang on. The next morning, her husband called Tahoun to tell her that her sister—25 and the mother of 2½-year-old Tasha—had died of a heart attack during the night. She weighed 80 lbs. "We couldn't believe it," says Toni's mother, Nina Johnson, now 75. "How could someone that young die like that?"

Determined that she would at least save herself, Tahoun continued seeing Dr. Robert Lynn Horne, a Las Vegas–based psychiatrist who specializes in eating disorders. She also began taking Prozac to counter the obsessive aspects of her personality. Tahoun—who lives in Vegas, around the corner from her mother and stepfather, when she's not flying—now follows a regimen of meditation and in times of stress keeps a daily food diary. "When a patient is in the anorectic phase," says Dr. Horne, "they tend to overestimate what they eat. Someone like Toni might think she's eaten 2,500 calories in one day, when in fact all she's eaten is 300. If she keeps a record, she sees what she's really had." To maintain a healthy weight, Tahoun needs to consume at least 1,600 calories a day.

Horne has helped in other ways. "We've worked with Toni on her feelings of low self-esteem," he says, "and we've done a lot of work helping her realize she was not responsible for her sister's death."

Even so, Tahoun has relapsed. When her weight drops dangerously, as it last did in 1996, Horne has her hospitalized for supervised feeding and psychiatric treatment. "I've been in and out of the hospital at least 10 times since 1987," she says. Weighing in at a healthy 128 lbs. today, Tahoun continues to fight her fear of being fat. "I think I'm pretty fat now," she says, "so I have to work on knowing that I'm not."

For Tahoun, there is no such thing as a cure; there is just the daily struggle. "I am an anorexic in remission," she says. "My mother has buried one child from this disease, and I can't do that to her again. I have to stay alive."

A Family Affair

When the three Battista children—Amy, Douglas and Jennifer—were growing up in New Castle, Pa., the family's kitchen housed a Weight Watchers cookbook, boxes of Sweet 'N' Low and cans of diet cola. The children's mother, Rudelle, 55, an elementary-school reading specialist, admits to her fat phobia. "We're an Italian family," she says. "As soon as you come into people's houses, it's like, 'Come in, have a cookie.' So I was always watching my weight."

Her children noticed. Says Amy, 32: "We all became good at dieting." As adolescents, she and Douglas, now 29, "would get on the scale and weigh each other," she says. And at age 9, Jennifer, now 28, wore a belt to bed "to keep my stomach flat."

Over the next several years, the siblings' behavior became even more troubling. At 14, the 5'6" Douglas—who felt insecure about his height and, he says, "lacked confidence about who I was"—began working out obsessively, pumping iron up to four hours a day. "I wanted to be buff and fit. I'd even shake my leg under my desk at school to burn calories."

At the same time, he started eating less, and in six months his weight fell from 120 lbs. to 80. Still, he says, "my midsection looked fat to me." His parents were similarly unimpressed by his weight loss. "He seemed to be getting taller while he was getting thinner," Rudelle says. "We just thought it was a growth spurt. We didn't think anything was wrong."

But when Douglas came home one day in May 1987 and told his mother he felt his heart was going to stop, she rushed him to the pediatrician—who diagnosed anorexia nervosa. "I had no idea what it was," says father Frank, 57, an engineer. "We didn't know if we had done something wrong."

Within days Douglas was admitted to a local psychiatric facility, where he underwent four months of inpatient group therapy. "I fought the treatment all the way," he says. "I was eating so I could get out."

Back home, Douglas resumed his old habits. After five months he weighed less than 90 lbs. and landed in the eating-disorders program at Johns Hopkins Hospital in Baltimore. It was a 10-hour round trip for Douglas's parents, who joined him once a week for six months in therapy. At one session, "Douglas became angry at something we said, walked out and slammed the door," Rudelle recalls. "The therapist said, 'Don't follow him. Go home.' We did, and from that time on, he came to realize that he had to take control of his problem."

Rudelle and Frank realized they had to take responsibility as well. "With anorexia there's clearly a learned pattern, like substance abuse," says Dr. Angela Guarda, who heads the Hopkins program. "When parents make comments that the less you weigh the better, it can be a trigger."

Suffering Sisters

By the time Douglas, weighing a healthy 125 lbs., returned home in April 1988, the diet foods and cookbooks were gone. Unfortunately the changes came too late to help Amy, who had started starving herself in high school, around the time Douglas entered Hopkins. "My brother was ill, and my family was torn apart," she says. "Things just got the better of me."

Her parents, now alert to the symptoms, tried to get her to eat. "Since she was a cheerleader, we told her if she lost weight, she couldn't cheer," Rudelle says. That didn't work. Amy struggled with her disorder until February 1996. Down to about 90 lbs., she checked into Hopkins. "I didn't spiral down like Douglas did," she says. "I just never was where I should have been weight-wise."

After a month of group and individual therapy as an inpatient, Amy spent six weeks living in the hospital's halfway house. There, in addition to participating in therapy that focused on food issues, she cooked, shopped for groceries and ate in restaurants—all to prepare her to reenter society.

Around that time, Jennifer, then 24, moved to Baltimore to teach elementary school, a job she still holds. Separated from family and friends, she says, "I didn't know what to do with myself." Like her siblings, she fixated on food. "I used to eat onions, sliced like an apple, and dip them in mustard, which has no fat," says the 5'1" Jennifer. Without her parents around, her anorexia became full-blown; by the summer of 1998, her weight had dropped from 113 to 83 lbs.

After repeated entreaties from her family, Jennifer checked herself into Hopkins that July, moving into the halfway house two months later. "The turning point was looking around and realizing that everyone in the group was doing worse than me," Jennifer says. "I saw the other girls as being out of control, and it just clicked."

Today Jennifer checks in at a healthy 111 lbs., a weight she has kept since early 2000. She still hesitates when it comes to eating fats, but, with the support of a therapist she sees every two weeks, she makes sure to eat 2,000 calories a day. "Food is an issue we can't ignore," says her husband, restaurant-kitchen assistant Seth Michaels, 26. "But if she's not in check, I'll tell her."

Douglas, too, still has anorexic thoughts. "They don't ever go away," he says. But thanks to therapy, Douglas—who is single and works as a human-resources manager for Disney in Pasadena—has maintained his 140-lb. weight for five years. "I'm in control now," he says.

Only Amy, a married mother of two in York, Pa., still struggles. She refuses to say what her weight is, other than that it's stable, and she continues individual therapy at Hopkins once a month. "I know where I was 15 years ago, and I've come a long way," Amy says. "But I'm not there yet."

CHAPTER 4

OVERCOMING EATING DISORDERS

EATING DISORDERS: RECOVERY IS POSSIBLE

Charles Montgomery

Just a few decades ago, Charles Montgomery reports, the medical profession had few resources for treating patients with eating disorders: Anorexia and bulimia were not well understood, and recovery rates were discouraging. However, he explains, the outlook for patients with eating disorders is far more optimistic today. In particular, Montgomery discusses the work of Jim Kirkpatrick, a Canadian physician who specializes in the treatment of people with eating disorders. According to the author, Kirkpatrick has made fundamental changes in the standard treatment model for eating disorders, thus improving patient outcomes and making recovery a real possibility. Montgomery is a freelance writer based in Vancouver who contributes to such magazines as *Canadian Geographic, Canadian Business*, and *Chatelaine*.

Dr. Jim Kirkpatrick had crossed paths with people with eating disorders for years before he treated his first case.

Back in the 1970s he was a musician playing bass guitar and flute in a travelling band. There was a dancer with the band, a charming, vivacious woman who nevertheless lost weight to the point of emaciation.

Years later, while working on a psychiatric ward during training at the University of Saskatchewan college of medicine, he met several young women admitted because of their struggles with anorexia nervosa. Then, during an outpatient psychiatric rotation, he saw a woman diagnosed with bulimia. She explained that she could eat huge amounts of food then simply purge it back out again.

The encounters left Dr. Kirkpatrick bewildered, amazed and feeling helpless to assist any of the women. Then, in 1988, after establishing a family practice in Victoria, B.C., he met the patient who would change his life: a young woman who seemed to have both anorexia nervosa and bulimia. She was extremely thin, would vomit frequently and was experiencing all the physiological symptoms of starvation.

Charles Montgomery, "Eating Disorders: Recovery Is Possible," *Medical Post*, vol. 27, September 18, 2001, p. 17. Copyright © 2001 by Charles Montgomery. Reproduced by permission.

"With her I realized the utter lack of resources for people with eating disorders. There was simply nothing there for her," says Dr. Kirkpatrick. "I had to decide whether to tackle this problem or leave it alone. In spite of the fact that there was so little known about eating disorders and so few resources available, I decided to take on the challenge."

A Leader in Treatment

Now 50, the Goose Bay, Labrador born doctor has treated more than 500 patients with eating disorders in his adopted home province of British Columbia, and has become a champion of their right to professional care.

In 1989 he helped found the British Columbia Eating Disorders Association. Its lobbying has helped make the province a world leader in the treatment and care of people with eating disorders. In February 2001, Dr. Kirkpatrick, along with Ontario family physician Dr. Paul Caldwell, published *Eating Disorders: Anorexia Nervosa, Bulimia, Binge Eating and Others*. The book is an A-to-Z guide for people affected by eating disorders and their caregivers, and provides a ray of hope that recovery is, indeed, possible.

The book examines recent research that suggests, in rare cases, eating disorders may be triggered by dementia, head injuries and even staphylococcus infection. It also notes that some people may have a genetic predisposition to eating disorders. Moreover, it reinforces the notion that the key elements of recovery from eating disorders are nutrition, weight gain, and changing patients' beliefs about eating and their bodies.

His own treatment model has evolved in two fundamental ways in recent years, Dr. Kirkpatrick says, partly because recovery must involve cognitive change in patients. "We are becoming more lenient in a way," he says. "It used to be that when people with eating disorders were in hospital programs, we would try to keep them there, sometimes for months on end, until we saw some improvement. The patient wouldn't necessarily be better off after that time. In fact, the experience might cause them to avoid treatment in the future. Now, our philosophy is to let them go and focus on treating them when they are ready."

Dr. Kirkpatrick now measures success differently, too. "Even if there is a lot of resistance to treatment in terms of changing the patient's behaviour, we can still improve quality of life," he says. "For example, we might start with someone who is binging and vomiting five times a day, who is critically underweight, on welfare, is suicidal and can't go to school. After six months, that person might still be binging and purging, but their weight may be improving, they may be back at school, off welfare and no longer suicidal. That's a better life, regardless of whether we've seen a lot of improvement with the eating disorder behaviour."

A Lack of Resources and Training

The greatest challenge in dealing with eating disorders in Canada and around the world remains lack of resources and trained caregivers, says Dr. Kirkpatrick. That means any doctor who makes the effort to learn more is likely to be swamped by patients.

"Some caregivers are afraid to treat people with eating disorders. Others resent having to treat them, because there is a lack of support," he says. So people with eating disorders get treated by professionals who are frustrated, overworked and who feel both inadequately skilled and under-supported.

The treatment can be a negative experience for the patients, their families and the people who treat them.

One solution is to educate all health-care professionals about the problem. "Nearly 100% of the people working in the area of eating disorders were never trained in the area during our formal studies. We all learn as we go along," says Dr. Kirkpatrick.

He and other colleagues at the international Academy of Eating Disorders (AED) are preparing to lobby professional colleges to help change that situation. "We need professionals to get training and experience before they get out of school: all medical doctors, all nurses, all therapists, all nutritionists, all occupational therapists and so on."

Beyond his work with the AED, Dr. Kirkpatrick has stepped aside from advocacy work in favour of focusing on clients. In the spring of 2001 he quit his general practice in Victoria, and now divides his time between a family planning centre and two Vancouver Island eating disorder programs.

A Sense of Purpose

"Working with (patients who have) eating disorders is immensely satisfying. It gives me the sense of purpose in medicine that I never found in general practice, partly because I am filling a need provided by so few caregivers. If any of us (caregivers) walked out, there would be nobody to replace us," says Dr. Kirkpatrick.

"And I do see all kinds of evidence of positive change. It's the really small things I notice. Subtle changes in attitude, like that moment when a patient decides she wants to get better, when she sees a glimmer of hope. Something in her has suddenly tweaked. Those are the rewarding times, and often they come when people have reached their darkest moments.

"There is an assumption in society and among some health professionals that people with eating disorders just don't get better. Well, they do get better. They do."

EFFECTIVE METHODS FOR THE TREATMENT OF EATING DISORDERS

Susan Ferraro

In the following selection, Susan Ferraro describes various methods of treating patients with eating disorders. Research has shown that in-patient hospital care is the best way to halt disordered eating behaviors, Ferraro reports. After a patient is released from the hospital, the author writes, individual or group therapy can be extremely beneficial, and family therapy is very important for adolescent sufferers. Other promising approaches include cognitive behavioral therapy and antidepressant medications, she explains. Health care professionals are also researching methods to prevent relapses—one of the main stumbling blocks in the road to recovery. Ferraro is a feature writer for the *Daily News*, a New York newspaper.

Too terrified to do something violent, Elizabeth R. set about killing herself by starvation. In December 2001, she weighed 52 pounds. She had entered the death zone of anorexia.

"My body started giving out," says Elizabeth, who is 23 years old and 5-feet-1. "It was, 'You are either going to die or get help.' I don't know how much I wanted to live, but there was my family. I came here. Now I want to live."

Elizabeth is an in-patient at the Eating Disorders Research Unit of the New York Psychiatric Institute (NYPI) in Manhattan. These days, she tips the scales at a triumphant 106 pounds.

Pizza, she admits, is still "scary," because it has so many calories. And her recovery program is "very strict. You come in and they put you on 1,800 calories a day! You eat it all or your activities are restricted, you can't go outside, and this is not a big place. Or if you do eat it all and still drop weight, they put you on bed rest."

But, she says, "These people pretty much raised me from the dead."

New research from the Renfrew Center Foundation, an eating disorders organization in Philadelphia with a branch in Manhattan, finds that residential treatment similar to Elizabeth's in-patient hospital care is the best way to stop anorexia and other eating disorders.

The all-out approach also sticks to the ribs longer, as patients are less likely to relapse. "It is known that in-patient care is clearly the most efficient," says Dr. Evelyn Attia at NYPI.

The need for help is "absolutely high," Attia says. At Elizabeth's program, there is a waiting list. While anorexia was long considered a disorder prevalent among affluent Caucasian teens, it is now on the rise in black, Hispanic and Asian populations, doctors say.

And the patients are getting younger. A decade ago, says Judith Rabinor, Ph.D., a New York and Long Island therapist who specializes in eating disorders, anorexics younger than 12 were rare. "Now they are common."

When Pounds Do Not Add Up

"Anorexia probably has the highest mortality of any psychiatric illness, including schizophrenia and depression," says Dr. Timothy Walsh, who heads NYPI's eating-disorders research unit. One in 10 may die over the long term.

A person is anorexic if her (or his) weight drops below 85% of what it should be, based on a body mass index of at least 18.5. (Officially, one begins to be overweight at a BMI of 26. Normal BMI ranges between 19 and 25.)

Ideal weight varies by height and build; Elizabeth's normal thin range is probably 105 to 110 pounds. The trendsetting 5-foot-6 Twiggy, who weighed 91 pounds when she became a '60s fashion icon, was about 79% of her minimum healthy weight of 115 pounds.

Officially, anorexia and bulimia (anorexia's binge-and-purge sister) affect few: Only 0.5% of Americans are anorexic and up to 4% are bulimic. But "a lot of people have bits" of eating-disorder behavior, says Walsh, and run a greater risk of pitching into serious trouble.

The typical patient is white and female, middle or upper class economically and, in personality, a perfectionist who is grasping for some control in an otherwise stressed and out-of-control life.

Women of color often have a protective ethnic culture that includes a beauty standard that favors larger women and celebrates being female, says Adrienne Ressler, a body-image expert at Renfrew.

But that shield dissolves as they leave the familiar to embrace "the idealism of popular culture," Ressler notes. If they tend toward eating disorders, those torn between cultures tend to become bulimic, and those who abandon the old are more likely to be anorexic.

Marcia Herrin, head of the Dartmouth College Eating Disorder Program, says that 70% of teens don't like their bodies, and every day about 66% of teen girls and 20% of teen boys are dieting.

In one study, 7% of boys and 13% of girls binged and purged "a few times a week and more," a problem that often co-exists with anorexia. Other researchers found that about one in three had bulimic-like "behaviors."

One reason: Well-publicized models and celebrities are thinner now than they used to be. "Young girls today think Marilyn Monroe was a pig, and Sophia Loren gross," says Ressler. "The beauty ideal today is very different, much harder to obtain and maintain."

Girls are most vulnerable, but men "are catching up," says Dr. Joseph Donnellan, head of the eating-disorders program at Somerset (N.J.) Medical Center. Males now account for about 20% of eating disorder patients, he says.

"They didn't used to have the pressure to look good," Donnellan explains, but "in the past 10 years there has been a proliferation of men's magazines with lean, muscled [models on the] covers."

Food Madness

On the face of it, anorexia is simply irrational—"A Starving Madness," as Rabinor titled her book of eating-disorder case histories.

No one knows what causes eating disorders, but they occur in societies where food is plentiful and, experts suggest, thinness is prized. The driving force is almost always intensely personal.

It's usually not boyfriends. As Walsh notes, studies show males choose curvier female silhouettes over skinny ones. But there are clear patterns of "biological, psychological and social causes," Donnellan says.

Twenty years ago, Lisa Karen dieted to drop the "freshman five" weight gained her first year at college. Karen, who is 5-feet-4½ inches, exercised constantly. She dropped to 110 pounds, then boomeranged to 155 pounds—borderline eating-disorder behavior.

When she was 36, for reasons she won't disclose, Karen suddenly dropped to 105 pounds, or 88% of a minimally healthy weight. Enough was enough: Karen spent most of 2000 in Donnellan's programs.

Today she weighs 126 pounds, slim but definitely healthy.

"Anything can trigger it," says Karen. "It can be losing a child, a friend. It can be sibling rivalry, an alcoholic or abusive relative, a parent who is just not there. But finally, one thing is the last thing.

"Your whole life is falling apart and you need to have control over something and you can control what you eat or don't eat. You can be a complete failure in the rest of your life, but you can be a complete success with this."

In New York, Elizabeth R. can tell exactly how stress and hurt led to self-destruction. She was date-raped at 15, somehow blamed herself and told no one. Full of self-loathing for her body, she began denying it food.

Because she thought she was "bad," she says, she ran with a tough crowd; recovering from a secret abortion, she brushed off a call from her sick grandmother and was wracked by guilt when her grandmother died the next day.

Again, she told no one.

A year later, a handsome, young (and married) high school teacher seduced her. She blamed herself. "I felt like I wanted to die. I was too much of a chicken to pull the trigger, so I started to starve myself to death."

As with all starving people, food consumed her thoughts.

Feeding the Solution

"Anorexia is an old illness, and a tough one to get over," says Walsh. But multifaceted therapies are getting results. "The nice thing is that many people do get well and live happily ever after, in completely normal lives."

The first step is to make sure there is no underlying physical illness, says Judith Brisman, Ph.D., head of the Eating Disorders Resource Center in New York.

If there is no medical problem, therapy is vital—especially if the disease is caught early in adolescents, says Walsh, when there is time for a real reversal.

One-on-one counseling can provide the support patients need to find their healthy selves. Or group therapy, which Rabinor often recommends, can be the key.

Hospitalization may be necessary. The Somerset program has psychiatrists, social workers, dietitians, occupational and art therapists, nurses and teachers who help keep students up on classwork, says Donnellan. Assorted forms of therapy at the NYPI force patients "to think, to stand up on your own," Elizabeth says to take responsibility for their health and drop not weight but years of bad feelings.

Among the most promising approaches, says Walsh:

• Family therapy for adolescents with anorexia. The disorder can tyrannize households—parents, for example, might require that everyone eat broccoli all the time because an ailing child insists on it. Counseling "helps parents get more in control," Walsh says, so a family can eat normal meals together, and kids "get the weight up or they can't be on the track team."

• Cognitive Behavioral Treatment. Patients identify triggers and patterns, write them down and bring their notes to therapy. "Hopefully, they will begin to think more rationally and behave more normally," Walsh says.

Changing thought patterns is difficult, but rehearsal helps. For instance, as they walk down the street, instead of thinking about bingeing and booting a few dozen cookies, patients train themselves to focus on a new project, says Brisman.

Storytelling can help, Rabinor says. Patients often have "unarticulated emotional vulnerabilities" that can emerge on the page, and "you can help someone write a new ending."

• Medication. Eating-disorder patients may benefit from antidepressants like Prozac, which can ease depression, which is sometimes linked to eating disorders. Since bad eating behaviors often follow bad feelings, being more upbeat may help stop or prevent relapses.

• Doctors are exploring the science of eating disorders, learning how and when the body's reactions change when, for example, extremely thin women stop having periods and suffer bone loss.

• Perhaps most promising, Walsh and others are studying relapse prevention.

The Gradual Process of Recovery

Elizabeth will be in the relapse prevention program after she leaves NYPI in April 2002, and in a followup Prozac study.

Now, after four failed attempts to halt her self-destruction, she is healing. The New York program has "brought me to a place where I can see the eating disorder as a disorder," and has helped her uncover hidden hurts and guilts—a painful process.

"But if I can make it here, I know there is a strong person in there," Elizabeth says.

Nothing is certain. "I'm not necessarily well," she says. "But I can tolerate where I am. I can cope in healthier ways with problems. I can be with people again. I can live my life. I am okay."

THE TREATMENT OF ANOREXIA: A CASE STUDY

Roger Verdon

Roger Verdon presents a case study of the treatment of anorexia nervosa in the following selection. The case study follows Nikki, a thirteen-year-old anorexic, after her admission to the Eating Disorders Program at the Menninger Clinic in Topeka, Kansas. Verdon emphasizes that eating disorders must be diagnosed quickly in order to ensure the best possible outcome. He explains that while researchers have yet to determine the most effective treatment methods, so far, an early and aggressive approach seems to work best. Individualized treatment tailored to the needs of each patient is also beneficial, he maintains. In Nikki's case, her eating disorder seems to have been triggered by a strep infection—an unusual cause that points out the importance of identifying and treating any underlying physical conditions. Verdon is the senior editor of the *Menninger Perspective*.

When Nikki arrived at Menninger, she was a good student and a fine daughter from a loving family. In Nikki's view, she had only one problem: she was too fat. Never mind that she had shed 30 pounds in recent months from her already thin frame. What she saw in the mirror was an imperfect body. She feared getting fatter; consequently, she was reluctant to eat.

Her arrival at Menninger earned her a certain notoriety. She would now be counted among a select and growing group throughout the nation whose members have an eating disorder: 10 out of every 100 American females at some time in their life, according to the American Academy of Child and Adolescent Psychiatry. Boys also suffer the disorders, but much less often.

That Nikki's disorder was diagnosed as anorexia nervosa is notable, since it has among the highest mortality and morbidity rates of all psychiatric illnesses. "That means," said Dr. Mae Sokol, a Menninger eating disorders expert who would treat Nikki, "that more people die of it or derive medical problems from it than any other psychiatric disorder. It is a very deadly disease." Among other things, a major ini-

Roger Verdon, "Mirror, Mirror, on the Wall, Who Is the Thinnest of Them All?" *Reclaiming Children and Youth*, vol. 9, Fall 2000, p. 157. Copyright © 2000 by Pro-Ed. Reproduced by permission of the author.

tial concern for Nikki's Menninger treaters was to halt her increasing emaciation and get her weight up. That would be the course of treatment if everything went smoothly, and if Nikki's aversion to food didn't defeat her own best efforts and those of her therapists.

Nikki's family voiced high hopes. So did her treatment team, whose members were prepared to do whatever was required to save her life. But the situation posed its own conundrum, as do so many physical and mental disorders. If Nikki didn't eat, she could die. And Nikki's greatest fear was gaining weight. Nikki, herself, would have to play a major role in her own recovery. Everyone was counting on her. In her whole life, Nikki might never confront such a difficult challenge, an enormous task for anyone at any age, but perhaps especially for Nikki, who was all of 13 years old.

Early Is Better

Most eating disorders are treatable, and many young people have been placed back on the road to health. But swift action is called for. An eating disorder left untreated is a dangerous condition.

Comprehensive treatment is recommended and requires a multi-disciplinary team approach that may involve individual, cognitive-behavioral and family therapies, direct work with psychiatrists and psychotherapists, group psychotherapy, biofeedback, nutrition, and medication. The Menninger Eating Disorders Program, which began in 1973, is a completely individualized treatment. The goal is to stabilize medical symptoms, examine underlying biological, emotional, social, spiritual, and mental issues, and develop a healthier lifestyle. The program diagnoses and treats children, adolescents, and young adults of both sexes evidencing the following disorders:

- Anorexia nervosa, which is characterized by self-starvation and often some form of overactivity or overexercise. A person with anorexia has a disturbed body image, an intense fear of becoming obese, and an inability to maintain normal body weight.
- Bulimia nervosa, signified by recurrent episodes of binge eating followed by purging. A person with bulimia tends to binge on high-calorie, easily ingested foods, and is preoccupied with body shape and weight. Regular purging behavior (such as self-induced vomiting, use of laxatives or diuretics, strict dieting or fasting), or rigorous exercise in order to prevent weight gain, accompanies this disorder.
- Compulsive overeating, distinguished by eating more than is nutritionally necessary, resulting in obesity. Many medical and psychological consequences often accompany compulsive overeating.
- Activity disorders entail sole reliance on excessive exercise to maintain desired weight, self-esteem, or calmness. Health, school, and relationships are often compromised as the individual pursues unrealistic goals for "fitness."

Lengths of stay differ with each patient, and a full continuum of care is available, including inpatient, day hospital, and outpatient services. Because of the severe nature of Nikki's condition, she required inpatient care. Since the average healthy range for a supervised weight gain is about 2 pounds per week, and she required a minimum weight gain of at least 20 pounds, Nikki and her family could anticipate 10 to 12 weeks of treatment, perhaps more, depending on her response and the severity of her physical and mental condition.

Starvation Diet

Dr. Mae Sokol has been examining the mental and physical effects of eating disorders for years. As the director of the Eating Disorders Program at Menninger, her work has resulted in important breakthroughs in the field, but even she finds her mostly young, mostly female anorexia nervosa patients somewhat mystifying: "Even when they are emaciated, these kids keep up their grades. They tend to be straight A students, perfect little girls quietly starving themselves to death. That's the stereotype. Their condition affects their cognitive abilities but not their abilities to do math and schoolwork. It's a different kind of cognition. It doesn't make any sense."

Solving the puzzle of how to treat each patient individually is how Dr. Sokol and her team spend their day. The rise of eating disorders has given Menninger clinicians a breadth of experience in some of the most extreme cases. Yet, identifying the best treatment method can still be as challenging as interpreting an ancient script.

Long-Term Effects

Too often in the short-term, the appearance of eating disorder symptoms may trouble a family, but not enough for them to intrude into a young girl's obsession with weight control. Some parents may simply write off such behavior as a phase in the developing life of a young person. That, of course, would be, and is, a grave mistake. Ignoring the signs of anorexia nervosa and bulimia may have long-term and devastating effects on a young person's developing body.

"If you don't grow normally when you're 12 or 14 years old, you may never have that window of opportunity to do it again," Dr. Sokol said, "and your reproductive organs may not develop normally, your bones may not have enough calcium, and these may turn out to be lifelong problems. There is a window of opportunity for human growth and no one knows what it is. It's different for each individual. The best thing to do is treat an eating disorder early and treat it aggressively. The vast majority of cases improve. The individual is then likely not to relapse in the future. Treatment will limit long-term damage to a developing body."

Unfortunately, the practice of starving oneself may be only the beginning of a vicious cycle. In fact, the disorder points to a shift in which the mind is concentrated on the body's outer appearance, to the exclusion of the entire landscape of the inner self. That's not a surprising consequence of abstaining from food. Improper nutrition results in a reduction of physical and mental functioning. That can mean impaired thinking and the eventual unraveling of a myriad of defenses that would otherwise stem the course of self-inflicted starvation. "We really think that malnutrition causes some brain damage," Dr. Sokol said, "and people can't think straight or it causes brain dysfunction. A lot of the behaviors our patients have is from the malnutrition created by their disorder." That can drastically alter how people—whether it's a 13-year-old girl or an adult male—view themselves and their world.

A Government Study

Research can be instructive about how malnutrition, as a consequence of starvation, affects mood and behavior. Dr. Ansel Keys, the man who developed and gave his name to K-rations, the military's field food supplies, spent 3 months overseeing the supervised starvation of a volunteer group of conscientious objectors in order to learn the effects of starvation on the human body and mind. Conducted in the waning days of World War II, the objectives of the government study were not meant to be punitive. There was a humanitarian and scientific interest in learning the effects of human starvation to better understand and treat returning prisoners of war and Holocaust survivors.

As recounted in Menninger psychiatrist Dr. Kathryn Zerbe's landmark book, *The Body Betrayed: Women, Eating Disorders, and Treatment*, Dr. Keys guided the healthy male subjects in losing one quarter of their body weight, which resulted in slowing down individual heart rate, respiration, and body temperature, conditions that replicate symptoms experienced by eating disorder patients. As they starved, their main topic of discussion became food, a common behavior among anorectic patients. But there were other similar behaviors, as well. Mealtime for the test participants became the focal point of the day, to the exclusion of all other activities. When they did eat, the men spiced their food excessively or mixed food groups on their plates. Some of the men, who occasionally slipped in self-control and overate, endured great guilt. Others who slipped developed a bingeing-purging disorder in an effort to remain loyal to the goals of the study.

At the onset of starvation, the research subjects grew irritable and angry and were beset by emotional difficulties, including depression, anxiety, and a general physical malaise. One participant became so depressed over food that he exhibited suicidal tendencies and was removed from the study. "These men cut their food up into little pieces," Dr. Sokol said. "They did a lot of the same things our patients do. The thought is that a lot of the behaviors of these men was from the malnutrition."

Months after the conclusion of the 90-day experiment, the men were consumed with concerns over body shape and fat. "The parallel between anorexia nervosa and these experimental findings with volunteers shows how much starvation alone affects mood and behavior," Dr. Zerbe stated. "Consequently, any treatment must begin with gaining weight and changing nutritional patterns, because some of the apparently psychological effects may really be the result of starvation."

First Things First

At Menninger, Dr. Sokol set down the rules for Nikki, a seventh-grader who was able to continue her education throughout her treatment. She was initially given the conventional treatment applied to most patients. As Dr. Sokol said,

> with treatment team members trying to lovingly get her to eat. Telling her how important it was. Telling her we know it's hard, but at the same time being very structured about it, setting limits. Saying things like: "Look, you need to take care of your body to live. We're not going to let you let yourself die, so if you don't eat and drink food we're going to give you oral supplements. If you don't drink that and you become medically compromised, we will give you an NG tube."

A "nasal-gastric" (NG) tube is inserted up the nose and into the throat. It is uncomfortable, and for patients concerned about their outer appearance, it looks awful. (In visually focused anorexia nervosa patients such concerns are not taken lightly.)

In the collegial group environment that exists among inpatients in the eating disorders program, veteran patients will always advise newcomers like Nikki that eating anything is preferable to coming within proximity of an NG tube. The peer pressure that can be brought to bear is a useful weapon the clinician exploits as often as possible. "One of the things that helps us in treatment is the group of kids together," Dr. Sokol said, "the pressure the kids put on one another. That's one of the things I love about my work. You put all these kids with anorexia together and they really get each other better. The kids who are in advanced treatment will help the ones who are struggling and they get positive results."

Among fellow high achievers, Nikki was encouraged to use her own competitive energies in a positive direction. Instead of seeking approval from her anorectic peers as the thinnest patient, for instance, her efforts might be redirected into becoming a volunteer member of the "junior staff," which entitles the recipient to help fellow patients who are not doing as well. The sense of purpose derived from such an exercise pays dividends in self-esteem and affirms the program's goals.

"Nikki was given the basic limits most eating disorder patients are presented," said Dr. Sokol, "eat, don't throw up, make sure no one throws food away, you need to gain weight in a structured environment, and you need to follow the structure to get better." Nikki went through the motions of conforming to the discipline, eventually gaining 20 pounds, despite holding firm to her radical ideas about eating. She remained horrified about gaining weight. On her plate she carefully put food at positions equivalent to an hour hand on a clock, placing morsels at the 3-, 6-, 9-, and 12-o'clock positions. She ate one piece at a time. Of 20 pieces of macaroni on her plate, she would have to eat 1 piece from each hour, and then go around the plate once again.

"That was very obsessive ideation," Dr. Sokol said. "Our patients are very similar to people with obsessive-compulsive disorder. They have obsessions about food and compulsions about exercise and about calories and how they eat their food. They tend to cut up their food into tiny pieces, and Nikki did this too. It could take her 2 hours to eat a meal." Consequently, Nikki's progress was minimal. "You could tell she was going to relapse the moment she got home," Dr. Sokol concluded. And the underlying cause of her condition remained elusive.

The Why Behind the Disorder

Pick any of a hundred reasons why an American teenager living in the most bountiful country on earth would restrain from eating, and you might not even come close. Eating disorders do not surface out of thin air; they have roots, and often they can be traced to various branches sprouting from the family tree. In addition to genetics as a factor behind the disorder, there may be underlying biochemical, behavioral, or environmental factors, or any combination thereof.

Anorexia nervosa may be the expression of conflicts over sexuality or a reaction to grief, or a way of expressing feelings during stressful or changing times. People with eating disorders share common traits: fear of getting fat, low self-esteem, helplessness. Many are perfectionists in an imperfect world, and the disorder manifests itself as a means of assuming some control over one aspect of life, or as a means of handling anxiety. Dr. Sokol and the treatment team continued to search for the motivation behind Nikki's loss of appetite. Something else had to be causing her aversion to food, maybe something that wasn't even in the medical literature. Dr. Sokol would have to probe deeper. What she found would not only change Nikki's life, it would also change Dr. Sokol's life.

Reviewing the Past

When her parents were asked when the eating disorders began, their answers were very specific. They gave dates concerning the onset of the disorder that were only days apart. "They agreed what made the moment memorable was the sudden onset of Nikki's worry over food." And not just the remarkable onset of worry, but the dramatic change in Nikki's appreciation of food. This attitude seemed to have appeared in an instant. Her behavior was an anomaly. Most eating disorders are gradual in nature.

"In the past, according to her parents, she was a little bit worried about food and calories," Dr. Sokol recalled.

> Like other young girls in our society she would say "Oh, I'd like to lose a few pounds, I want to be thin, I want to look like the models," but nothing unusual. And then, suddenly, she became very afraid of eating. She thought if she ate too much she would become extremely fat, and actually thought she was fat at the time. She was very, very upset.

Before arriving at Menninger, Nikki's poor eating habits had put her in a hospital several times for dehydration. Pediatricians fed her fluids intravenously and treated her but missed the eating problem. Consequently, Nikki would return home and relapse. Eventually, Nikki's parents put her in the psychiatric unit of a hospital. "They didn't know what to do with her," Dr. Sokol recounted. "They don't have the kind of structure we have. They did talk to her about her thoughts and feelings, but that's not all it's about. And at the point where they're not eating, and they're so terrified of eating, you can't really talk to them about their thoughts and feelings, anyway."

Then the parents mentioned a part of the story they hadn't previously disclosed. Three to four weeks prior to the onset of Nikki's eating disorder, everyone in her family had suffered sore throats. The flu-like symptoms kept everyone home. At the time, no one in the family received medical attention. The news set off warning bells. Dr. Sokol performed lab tests. Nikki's physical condition was consistent with strep.

A Very Bad Trip

Normally, when strep throat arises, the body's infection-fighting apparatus prepares to set sail. White blood cells produce antibodies which are directed to the infection in a natural process. But sometimes those same cells fall victim to "molecular mimicry," an incidence of navigational mischief that misdirects their geography off-course and toward molecules in the body disguised as the targeted infection. Once deceived by this "mimicry," if the heart is the mistaken destination, rheumatic fever results, which can then lead to rheumatic heart disease, a condition that attacks the heart. Once there, what began as a well-intentioned trip becomes an invasion of the brain's center—the basal ganglia—where human emotions are centered and influenced and psychiatric symptoms result. The long-winded theory behind this case of "mistaken identity" is called Pediatric Autoimmune Neuropsychiatric Disorders Associated with Streptococcus, also known by the acronym PANDAS.

When Dr. Sokol and her treatment team detected the proximity in time between the illness in Nikki and her family with the onset of Nikki's psychiatric symptoms, antibiotics were prescribed. "It was very interesting," Dr. Sokol said. "She didn't appear to have an acute infection, but just by taking the antibiotics she started getting better. Within 2 weeks, her thinking cleared up." In some rare cases, like Nikki's, PANDAS has been linked with anorexia nervosa, obsessive-compulsive disorders, and tics or abnormal body movements. As Nikki improved physically and mentally, she began to benefit from intensive individual psychotherapy.

One More Time

Although the cause of Nikki's anorexia nervosa may have been novel, the condition manifested itself in all its conventional phases. After her release from Menninger, she eventually went off antibiotics. Months later, she again came down with strep, and the same thoughts that plagued her under the daunting grip of anorexia nervosa returned. Fortunately, she didn't stop eating. In fact, she was so worried about a relapse that she overate to compensate for her troubling thoughts. After consulting with Dr. Sokol, who prescribed antibiotics to Nikki and reassurance to her family, the strep cleared up, and so did Nikki's fears.

While anorexia nervosa's origins can be traced to the complexity of individual and family dynamics, conflicts and struggles, the cultural desire for a "perfect" body shape, infections, or a plethora of other causes, the research is only beginning. Dr. Sokol's solution to Nikki's case has become a part of medical literature, accepted as one cause for anorexia nervosa under the practice guidelines of the American Psychiatric Association. Meanwhile, Menninger research into the causes and treatment of eating disorders continues. "We don't have—and we're unlikely to find—any single cure," Dr. Sokol said. "We don't have a medicine that will take anorexia nervosa or any of the eating disorders away, and we don't have a single treatment that will take it away. We're really at a frontier."

CAN HEALTH CARE PROFESSIONALS WHO HAVE HAD EATING DISORDERS EFFECTIVELY HELP OTHERS?

Kate Jennison

In the following article, Kate Jennison examines the debate among eating disorder experts as to whether people who have suffered from eating disorders in the past can be effective professionals in the field. Many health care professionals believe that individuals with a history of eating disorders may identify too strongly with the patients they are treating, thereby setting themselves up for a relapse, Jennison explains. Conversely, she writes, some experts maintain that a professional who has personal experience with eating disorders can relate to patients in ways that other health care providers cannot. While they may be vulnerable to relapse, Jennison concludes, these professionals bring a unique perspective to the recovery process that can be beneficial for the patients they work with. Jennison writes for the *National Post*, a Canadian newspaper.

"My eating disorder pretty much called me to this profession," says Erin Tiberio, a 26-year-old nutritionist in Baltimore, Md., and recovering bulimic. "At the time I was a psych major. . . . Go figure. . . . I was out running one day and I started thinking: Well, maybe if I learn how to feed other people, I'll be able to fix it somehow. I'll find out what went wrong, why I have the disorder. After my run I went straight up to my advisor's office and told him I was switching my major."

Tiberio's new major at the University of Pittsburgh was clinical dietetics and nutrition. "The whole program felt like a really good fit," she says. "People who have eating disorders like to know everything about food. I can remember when I was little just being fascinated by food. It's a fascination that's pretty much run my entire life."

"When I was in treatment for my eating disorder I remember telling my mum that being a dietitian was something I would really want to do," says Jennifer Schulte, a dietitian at Laureate Psychiatric Hospital's Eating Disorder Clinic in Tulsa, Okla. "After I'd recovered [from my eating disorder], I forgot about the idea until it was time for me to go to college. But I knew then that was what I wanted to do."

"It's strange," says Simone Berger, a 27-year-old nutritionist with her own eating disorder clinic in Thornhill, Ont., "but the whole time I had anorexia I had my head on for certain things. I would take myself off to the doctor regularly to have my blood work done to make sure I was OK. And I always had this awareness of and interest in nutrition and health. I felt like this pull to study it."

A History of Eating Disorders

Stories like Tiberio's, Schulte's and Berger's are not uncommon among nutritionists and eating disorder professionals. As the stigma around eating disorders lessens and research on the subject grows, an increasing number of workers in the field are admitting that they too once had an eating disorder.

"But it's not something that I just randomly [blurt] out the first time I meet my patients, you know. 'Oh hello, I'm Jenny, your nutritionist and a former anorexic,'" continues Schulte. "There are times when it comes up. When I feel like it's an encouragement tool. When there's something my patient is struggling with around their eating disorder and I think it would help them to know. Then I tell them."

"It's the first thing I tell my clients," says Berger. "I truly don't believe that somebody understands how someone's feeling when they are going through an eating disorder unless they've been there themselves. So I let them know right away that I've been there. I know what they're going through."

The theory that eating disorder sufferers are best served when the nutritionists, counsellors and nurses sitting across from them can say, "I was once you. I got to the other side. You can, too" is not one all eating disorder experts are comfortable with. Reaction to the new constituency of "recovered" professionals in the field is mixed, ranging from enthusiasm to outright suspicion. There is, in fact, growing concern that some of these professionals might not be as "recovered" as they like to think they are.

The Risk of Relapse

"If you have had an eating disorder, you're vulnerable for life," says Dr. Angela Guarda, director of the Eating and Weight Disorders Program at Johns Hopkins Hospital in Baltimore.

"And if you look at the statistics on outcome for eating disorders, they're not great. Twenty-five per cent at most of patients with anorexia recover. So now this supposed army of nutritionists and counsellors are all, one presumes, in that 25%—and that's people who just recover to normal dieting levels. It doesn't mean they're truly recovered. It just means they don't meet the criteria for an eating disorder . . . they don't have a fear of fatness that's excessive and they aren't underweight."

According to Guarda, because anorexia and bulimia are "driven" (addictive) behavioural disorders, they are also cue-driven. "Which means," she says, "when you talk to someone else who engages in the behaviour, you kind of get excited about it yourself. So while, yes, [if you're that nutritionist or counsellor with a history of an eating disorder] you can walk in the eating disorder patient's shoes in the way that maybe somebody who has never experienced an eating disorder can't. You are also at greater risk of literally walking in their shoes—that is, of falling back into your old eating disorder behaviours."

The interest many eating disorder sufferers have in studying nutrition is, it seems, commonly encountered by eating disorder professionals. According to Guarda, the interest stems from the patients' desire to "figure themselves out."

"And I think it's natural for humans in distress to want to figure out their problems," she says.

A Symptom of Eating Disorders

But Ann Kerr, who is the director of the eating disorder program at Toronto's Sheena's Place, argues that the eating disorder sufferer's interest in nutrition is more often symptomatic of the eating disorder.

"When you're hungry, all you can think about is food," says Kerr. "And the eating disorder patient is always hungry. Hungry for information about food, hungry to think about food, hungry to find out answers about food. . . . So studying nutrition [for the eating disorder patient] is more often than not a substitute for eating."

Kerr says that when she began hiring staff for the eating disorder program at Sheena's Place in 1996, she chose the most highly qualified, most sensitive people she could find. Because it is illegal in both Canada and the United States to ask an applicant if they've ever had an eating disorder, all of her staff were hired without any knowledge on her part of whether they did or did not have a history of eating disorders. Since 1996, however, Kerr has discovered that from a third to half of her staff have had the eating disorders they are now, with her assistance, treating.

"When some of my staff confided in me," says Kerr, "I was surprised. I just would have had no idea that they had ever had an eating disorder. And I think in most professional communities . . . people would have been much more cautious about disclosing it. Because they would be too worried about how people like me who were employing them would react. But I'm positive on the whole issue. I think it's very important that people who have recovered from an eating disorder should be able to work in this area without any sense that it's a problem."

Making the Problem Worse

Guarda disagrees. "Anyone who said to me, 'I'm recovered now and I want to go into the nutrition field and counsel eating disorder patients,' I would counsel them against it," she says. Guarda adds that her own professional experience in the field has taught her to be cautious about recovered eating disorder staff who are working with eating disorder patients.

"I've seen many students and several nurses and other people on my staff with histories of eating disorders get sicker when they've started working with the eating disorder population," says Guarda. "And it affects the patients because they start commenting on it. I've had patients come to me and say, 'One of your staff has anorexia and she's trying to treat us,' and well, when it happens, it's a very awkward problem."

Erin Tiberio has been one of those "awkward" problems. When she graduated with her bachelor of science degree in clinical dietetics and nutrition, her bulimia was at its worst.

"The first job I had as a dietitian was brutal," she says. "I was doing a lot of different meal planning for people and I felt like a huge hypocrite. I kept feeling: Here I am trying to give these people sound nutritional advice when I'm sticking my fingers down my throat at night."

For years, Tiberio says, she had kept notebooks about how much she ate. "I would weigh myself every day and keep account of how many calories I had to burn off when I exercised. So when I started to keep notebooks on other people and weighing them, it was so overwhelming and repetitive that it just kept bringing me back to the place [where she would be throwing up between seven and 11 times a day]. I couldn't do it and be well."

She thought her situation might improve if she transferred into a nutritional support services job at Johns Hopkins Hospital. "It's tube feeding and intravenous. Everything is commercially prepared and is ordered from a company so it doesn't look like food," says Tiberio. But in spite of the transfer to the more scientific job, she still couldn't cope. Her eating disorder landed her in the hospital in January, 2002.

"I wound up in emergency twice for dehydration," she says. "They didn't admit me at first. They said I could be an outpatient." But her health worsened and she eventually had to be admitted into the same hospital she worked for. "I still feel embarrassed," she says. "And when I first got out of the hospital, I felt terrible going back to work. Everybody in my workplace knew. Here I was, supposedly representing this field of nutrition, and meanwhile I was being hospitalized for bulimia.

"And I guess," she adds, "I don't think you can ever really say with something like an eating disorder, 'I'm fully recovered.' I think it's something you have to work at every day so you don't get dragged back into it. These are behaviours that have been ingrained in our minds since very early on. And it's a lot of work to stop the behaviour and get back on the right track."

Motivation to Stay Healthy

Jennifer Schulte acknowledges that for some eating disorder specialists with a history of eating disorders, there is a danger that the job could, as it did for Tiberio, trigger old behaviours. But she feels that in her case the opposite is true.

"I look at my patients," says Schulte, "and I think, 'Oh boy, do I ever need to keep on eating fat.' They keep me motivated to stay healthy, to stay eating right."

Simone Berger agrees. "I see my clients and it's really, really sad. I never ever want to be there again. And I think recovery depends on the person. If somebody wants to be recovered, they can be. And if people aren't fully recovered from their eating disorder, what I've found is they actually don't like talking about it. So, I mean, if I wasn't fully recovered, would I really want to be dealing with people with eating disorders? No. Would I really want to be sharing my story? No. Would I want to look at anorexic clients all day? No. Because I would be comparing my weight to my client's weight."

One of the issues currently being debated in the field is the time frame for establishing that someone is in fact fully recovered from an eating disorder. Those on the conservative side of the debate, such as Guarda, estimate it takes a good five to 10 years for full recovery from an eating disorder. Other experts, such as Dr. Craig Johnson, director of the Eating Disorders Program at Laureate Psychiatric Hospital, favour a figure closer to two years.

"Minimally we would look to someone having at least two years of very solid recovery before they enter into the eating disorder nutritional field," says Johnson.

The Benefits of a History of Recovery

Johnson, who has been in the field for 20 years, has since 1989 actively tried to hire dietitians and clinical staff with a history of recovery.

"Because we have a reputation for being interested and open to people who have had personal recovery from an eating disorder, generally applicants will veer in the direction of letting us know if they've had an eating disorder during the interview process," says Johnson.

"And what we've found is that the best combination [staff-wise] is to have somewhere around a third of our staff that have personal recovery and the other two-thirds who don't. The two-thirds that don't sort of help keep the third that do from getting in more difficulty—and kind of watch out for them. And the third that have personal recovery teach the other two-thirds a lot more about the illness than you can read in a book."

Johnson argues that the automatic connection that is often established between the patient with anorexia and the nutritionist or counsellor who has had anorexia can in fact be invaluable to the patient's recovery process. He compares eating disorder professionals with a history of eating disorders to elite sports coaches. "Haven't most elite coaches been involved in some level with the sport they are coaching?" Johnson asks.

Still, he admits, there can be downsides to having staff who have recovered from eating disorders. "Sometimes people who have personal recovery [and who work in the eating disorder field] are actually on a mission," he says. "Meaning, they assume more responsibility for their patients' recovery than they should. They want the patient to recover more than the patient does. So they wind up working harder than the patient does to try to get them into recovery."

Part of the process of recovery, Johnson says, is letting the patient with the eating disorder struggle with his or her own willingness and ability to recover, so it is important that staff do not overcompensate.

And sometimes, it seems, the eating disorder professional with a history of eating disorders can be a little too myopic about the "correct" method of recovery, believing the method that worked for them is the only route to recovery—"and not be able to see," says Johnson, "that there are other ways to recover."

Nevertheless, Johnson is adamant that the commitment and sensitivity staff with their own experience of eating disorders bring to his hospital team is uniquely valuable to his patients.

Schulte agrees. "Without having had an eating disorder," she says, "I don't think I would be as good at what I do. I really don't. And I don't think I would be as passionate about it. I can see when my patients find out that I've had an eating disorder their whole tone changes. I can see an instant connection in their eyes that wasn't there before. They take me more seriously, and the trust is there."

"I love what I do, more than anything," says Berger. "I love dealing with my clientele. I love helping them. It's so rewarding. And just knowing what people are going through, I just want to get them out of it."

WAYS TO TUNE OUT DISTORTED MEDIA MESSAGES ABOUT BODY TYPES

Nancy Fitzgerald

Television can have a considerable influence on how teens feel about their appearance, writes Nancy Fitzgerald in the following selection. Fitzgerald notes that the thin actresses seen on television do not reflect the real world, where one in four women is overweight. Furthermore, she observes, overweight women on TV are generally not portrayed as attractive or successful. These distorted media messages can lead some teens to struggle to conform to an unrealistic ideal of thinness, putting them at risk for developing eating disorders, Fitzgerald points out. She suggests that teens can develop positive body images and avoid eating disorders by watching less TV, engaging in healthy exercise, focusing on internal qualities rather than external appearances, and enlisting help from like-minded friends. Fitzgerald writes for *Scholastic Choices* and *Careers & Colleges* magazine.

Ariel Jastromb was only a sixth-grader when she got her first subscription to *Vogue* magazine. A fashion lover, Ariel pored over the magazine's glossy pages and imagined how she'd look in the skimpy clothes that the models wore. Ariel tuned into TV shows like *Friends* and *Dawson's Creek*, where superthin actresses dressed in the latest styles and wound up with the cutest guys.

"To me, that was how everyone was supposed to look," Ariel says. "I'd watch the people on TV and think, Why can't I be like them? But when I tried on the kinds of clothes I'd see on television, they always looked wrong on me. I felt so fat. I didn't realize that leather miniskirts just don't look good on many people."

Ariel is right. Experts say that only one woman in 20,000 has the body type of the size-two actresses who populate the make-believe world of television. Most real-life women look a lot different. According to a recent Michigan State University study, one in four women is overweight—and only 5 percent are underweight.

Unreal TV

But in TV land, reality is flip-flopped. There, 10 percent of the women are overweight—and an amazing 33 percent are underweight. "TV is the biggest storyteller in our culture," says Vickie Rutledge Shields, a professor of telecommunications at Bowling Green State University in Ohio. "And the most consistent story it tells for girls is that if you can look like the cute girls on TV, everything else will fall into place. Girls get the message that their bodies should be tall and thin, and that appearance should be the focus of their lives."

That's how it was for Ariel, and it led to disaster. Her quest to look like the girls on TV caused her to go on a crash diet, which contributed to her developing the eating disorder anorexia nervosa. When she was a high school freshman, Ariel lost 45 pounds in a couple of months and was subsequently hospitalized for severe depression and bipolar disorder—the dangerous mood swings that often accompany anorexia.

"My grades plummeted and all I did was lock myself in my room," says Ariel, who lives in Highland Park, Illinois. "I couldn't concentrate and couldn't function without food. I was filled with self-loathing. I felt like I was less of a person because I didn't look good enough. I felt that no one could ever love me."

Dangerous Disorders

Ariel isn't alone. Nearly 750,000 high school students in the United States—most of them girls—suffer from anorexia, according to the Association of Anorexia Nervosa and Related Disorders. TV is a major part of the problem. Many teen girls end up believing that life should imitate art. "I used to watch *Beverly Hills 90210* and *Party of Five*," says Casey Schurr, 16, of Los Angeles. "The girls on those shows were the ideal girls. They had flat stomachs, perfect hair, skinny arms, and nice breasts. I'd think, I don't look like them, and figure that I would never appeal to any guy. I tore myself apart over it."

Guys fall for the trap as well, which heightens the pressure on girls. "I'll be sitting there watching TV with my boyfriend," says Tara Powell, 16, of Keene, New Hampshire. "He'll say, 'You should look like that.'"

The problem goes beyond the borders of the U.S. On the remote island of Fiji in the Pacific Ocean, television only became available in 1995. Just three years later, eating disorders among teenage girls living on Fiji had more than doubled. "Before television arrived, there was little talk of dieting," says media expert Jeanne Kilborn, author of *Can't Buy My Love*. "Telling a woman she had gained weight was considered a compliment. This says something about how powerful the images on TV really are."

A Role for Laughs

Not every woman on TV is thin. But overweight women are given only supporting roles. For instance, the tall and skinny girl is the star of the show while her chubby friend is the funny sidekick. "Look at Mimi on *The Drew Carey Show*," says Brittany Blount, 16, of Annville, Pennsylvania. "You know that she's only there to be mocked."

The Michigan State study showed that heavyset women on TV had fewer romantic relationships and were less likely to date. They are often older, unemployed, and the target of fat jokes. "Girls are getting the message that to be overweight is a life sentence to pain, shame, and sorrow," says Dr. Susan Hendrich, professor of psychology at Wichita State University in Kansas. "It's very subtle—nobody comes out and says fat girls don't get dates, but you see a crowd of young women, and the one getting attention from a man is the one who's tall and thin."

So is there any truth to the physiques you see on TV? Yes, and here it is: Actresses on TV and in the movies work hard to keep themselves thin. "Regular girls are comparing themselves with images of professionals who are doing enormous amounts of work to look that way," says Emily Vaughn, a family counselor in Los Angeles. Well-known TV actresses have personal trainers to help them tone their muscles, cooks to prepare low-calorie meals, hair stylists to keep their do's in place, and makeup artists to cover up all their imperfections.

Stop the Madness

So unless you've got an entourage to keep you looking good, don't compare yourself with Jennifer Aniston, Katie Holmes, or Sarah Michelle Gellar. "The comparison is always unnatural," says Shields. "When you continually compare yourself to something unrealistic, you feel depressed, guilty, and ashamed."

But turn on the TV and Rachel, Joey, and Buffy are there for you to gawk at. How can you fight the message TV is sending you? Here's a list:

• Turn off the TV, or at least cut down on how much TV you watch. The less you watch, the less you'll expose yourself to those ultra-thin bodies that are driving you crazy. It'll help to reduce how often you look at fashion magazines too.

• Exercise. Whether it's taking walks with your friends or joining an organized sport, breaking a sweat can help you feel good about yourself both physically and mentally. Studies show that there is a strong connection between sports and positive body image. "Girls can look to athletes as alternative role models," says Leslie Haywood, author of *Pretty Good for a Girl*. "Sports makes girls aware that there's a range of body types, and you don't have to fit one image."

• Focus on qualities you admire in real women. Forget about appearance. Write down the things you like about women you know. Chances are you appreciate their kindness, creativity, generosity, brains, and sense of humor—not their dress size.

• Think positively about yourself. Think about what you like about yourself. Maybe you're a good student, or have lots of strong friendships, or earn your own money by working part-time. Reminding yourself of what you're good at will help build self-confidence and belief in yourself.

• Enlist your friends' help. Your pals know you. They can remind you how great you are. And if you find that the people you hang out with are too obsessed with their bodies, maybe it's time to find some new friends.

Ariel Jastromb, now 16 and a junior in high school, turned her life around. Doctors helped her overcome her eating disorder. She decided to stop letting the media control how she feels about her body too. Ariel thinks other teens should do the same. "My advice is that you need to accept yourself, and others, for the way they are," Ariel says. "It sounds corny, but it's the only thing you can do. You can't control the media, but you can control yourself."

HELPING KIDS FORM A HEALTHY BODY IMAGE

Carol Weston

In the following article, Carol Weston stresses the importance of helping children form a healthy body image, which can greatly reduce the likelihood that they will develop an eating disorder. Peer pressure and media images can make kids self-conscious about how they look, Weston observes, but parents can combat this influence by praising their children's appearance. Parents should avoid sending kids mixed messages about their appearance, she cautions, and they may need to work on their own attitudes toward body weight. Finally, parents should talk to their kids about the natural weight gains that occur as their bodies prepare for the rapid growth that accompanies puberty, reassuring them that these changes are healthy and normal. Weston writes the column "Ask Carol" for *Girl's Life* magazine and is the author of *Teen Talk, Girl Talk*, and *For Girls Only*.

Recently, my ebullient daughter Emme, age eight, came home deflated.

"What's up?" I asked, though "What's down?" would have been nearer the mark.

She shrugged.

I hugged.

And I got my answer: A boy in school said she had big ears.

Well, guess what? Emme does have big ears. They run in the family. My older brother Eric was called Dumbo for years—usually by his closest friends.

I held Emme in my lap and told her she had big eyes and a big smile and a big heart, and yup, big ears too, and that I loved her exactly the way she was. We agreed that it wasn't very nice of that boy to pick on her and we wondered what was bugging him.

Emme scampered off—and I felt pretty good myself.

I hadn't denied what was true, nor had I rushed to discuss alternate hairstyles or future surgical options. I'd helped my beautiful daughter accept herself.

But her preteen and teen years lie ahead, and that almost surely means more and tougher battles with self-image. Because of peers, mirrors, and the media, kids are becoming increasingly self-conscious. Cosmetic surgery such as breast implants, tummy tucks, and liposuction is on the rise for those under 18. And out-of-control dieting is hurting younger and younger girls. "We're now seeing eating disorders not just among high school students but also in middle school students," says Claire Mysko, administrative director of the American Anorexia/Bulimia Association.

You can't change the world (at least not overnight), but you can make a difference in the way your child feels about his or her body. Here's how:

1. Praise, Praise, Praise. We've grown far too reluctant to compliment our children on their appearance, says Cecilia Ford, Ph.D., a clinical psychologist in New York who specializes in body image. "We shy away from saying 'You're so pretty' to little girls—but compliments are important, not antifeminist," she says. Of course, we don't want girls—or boys—to feel prized only because of good looks, but it doesn't compromise a child's intellect to say, "Cute ponytail," as well as, "You did a great job on that puzzle."

Boys thrive on compliments, too. When I was growing up, my family had a babysitter who never called my brother Eric or Dumbo. She called him Handsome. He recently confessed that it did wonders for his little ego. So praise away. You aren't setting your children up to be vain or shallow; you're helping them feel good about their bodies.

2. Indulge Power Rangers and Princesses. Your son wants to dress from head to toe in superhero gear? Your daughter likes to prance around in bright red lipstick and a dozen sparkly necklaces? Let 'em. Exaggerating gender stereotypes can help kids feel more secure in their bodies, says Ford. "Little boys feel small and weak, so they want to pretend they're huge and invincible," she says. For girls, dressing up is a way of trying out—and reveling in—their femininity. For both sexes, being allowed to adorn and enhance their bodies in a playful way instills a kind of pride of ownership that serves them well.

3. Beware of Sending Mixed Messages. If you tell your son his glasses look great, then ask him to remove them every time you point your Polaroid, what are you really saying? If you assure your daughter that her big nose has character, then remind her that she can get it fixed in a few years, what message are you sending? Children are not easily fooled.

Lisa Ackerman of Columbus, Ohio, has a 12-year-old daughter who, because of a medical emergency at birth, has no belly button. "Ever since she was a baby, I just told her she had a very special tummy. To tell you the truth, she became downright proud," Ackerman says. "So I sure wouldn't steer her away from a midriff blouse or a bikini." If someday her daughter isn't happy, Ackerman says she'd be open to discussing options—but she's not going to be the one to raise the issue.

Some parents are quick to suggest surgery to correct a child's "flaw," perhaps only with the intention of giving her every advantage in life. But as the advice columnist for *Girls' Life* magazine, I've received disconcerting letters like this one: "Dear Carol, My parents and doctor think I should have plastic surgery on my nose and ears. But I don't want to change myself for pure cosmetic reasons." I can't blame her. An extreme situation—disease, disfiguring injury—might indeed warrant surgery, or a young woman might eventually decide for herself that she wants to make a change. But parents should be wary of telling their kids they love them for their inner beauty, then pushing them toward physical perfection—when there is no such thing.

4. Make Peace with Your Own Body. If you moan about your thighs each time you look in the mirror, or if you leaf through magazines muttering, "I'd kill to look like that," your kids will begin to notice that you don't like your body. And because they identify strongly with you, there's a good chance they'll learn to find fault with their own bodies. After all, you're not only their role model, you probably share many of the same physical characteristics.

Set a good example. Even if you struggle with weight and body image, don't talk endlessly about your flaws. "When a mother obsesses about looks and dieting, kids pick up on it," says Ellyn Satter, a psychotherapist in private practice in Madison, Wisconsin, and author of *Secrets of Feeding a Healthy Family*. "What's more, when you have difficulty accepting yourself, it makes it harder for you to accept your child's shape. This in turn affects your child's self-esteem."

The more you care for and the less you curse your body, the healthier the message your children get. This also applies to moms and kids who worry about being too thin, not just those who see themselves as overweight. The focus should be on fitness, not on the scale and mirror. "If you have healthy habits, your kids will imitate them," says Lillie Rosenthal, a doctor of osteopathy who has run the New York Marathon. She suggests you let them see you enjoying walks or bike rides.

And when you do decide to treat yourself to an ice-cream cone? Don't blurt, "I'm such a pig!" or "That's half an hour on the StairMaster." Just enjoy it.

5. Arm Your Kids Against Eating Disorders. Yet regardless of how good an example you set, your daughter (or son) is going to be bombarded with unrealistic images of "ideal" bodies. And just when peer pressure is at an all-time high, a once-slim child might pack on pounds as a prelude to adolescence. This weight gain is actually necessary to support the hormonal changes of puberty. But a girl, especially, might panic about her changing shape.

You'll need to reassure her that the added flesh is normal, while many of the images she's seeing on television and in the movies aren't—and some are down-right fake. A national pilot program called Go Girls!, developed by the Seattle-based Eating Disorders Awareness and Prevention group, has counselors who go into schools and explain how photographs can be distorted or airbrushed and how the clothing on store mannequins and on many models must be pinned to fit properly. You might also want to discuss these ideas at home.

And be on the lookout for sudden weight loss or strange, ritualistic eating habits. If you suspect your daughter or son is willfully starving or is bingeing and vomiting, seek help immediately. Contact your pediatrician, the American Anorexia/Bulimia Association, or the National Eating Disorders Organization.

ORGANIZATIONS TO CONTACT

The editors have compiled the following list of organizations concerned with the issues presented in this book. The descriptions are derived from materials provided by the organizations. All have publications or information available for interested readers. The list was compiled on the date of publication of the present volume; the information provided here may change. Be aware that many organizations take several weeks or longer to respond to inquiries, so allow as much time as possible.

Academy for Eating Disorders (AED)
6728 Old McLean Village Dr., McLean, VA 22101
(703) 556-9222 • fax: (703) 556-8729
e-mail: aed@degnon.org • website: www.aedweb.org

AED was founded in 1993 with the purpose of bringing together professionals from multiple disciplines to work on finding effective treatments for anorexia, bulimia, binge-eating disorder, and related disorders. The academy promotes patient advocacy, research, prevention, and the dissemination of knowledge about eating disorders to professionals and the general public. Its publications include the quarterly *Academy for Eating Disorders Newsletter* and the *International Journal of Eating Disorders*.

American Academy of Child and Adolescent Psychiatry (AACAP)
3615 Wisconsin Ave. NW, Washington, DC 20016
(202) 966-7300 • fax: (202) 966-2891
website: www.aacap.org

A professional medical organization, AACAP serves as an advocate for the mental health needs of children, adolescents, and families. AACAP provides parents and families with information regarding developmental, behavioral, and mental disorders that affect children and adolescents. Among its publications are the fact sheet "Teenagers with Eating Disorders," the monthly *Journal of the American Academy of Child and Adolescent Psychiatry*, and the *Facts for Families* series.

American Psychiatric Association (APA)
1000 Wilson Blvd., Suite 1825, Arlington, VA 22209
(703) 907-7300
e-mail: apa@psych.org • website: www.psych.org

APA is an organization of psychiatrists dedicated to studying the nature, treatment, and prevention of mental disorders. It helps create mental health policies, distributes information about psychiatry, and promotes psychiatric research and education. APA publishes the monthly *American Journal of Psychiatry*.

American Psychological Association (APA)
750 First St. NE, Washington, DC 20002-4242
(800) 374-2721 • (202) 336-5500
e-mail: public.affairs@apa.org • website: www.apa.org

This society of psychologists aims to "advance psychology as a science, as a profession, and as a means of promoting human welfare." It produces numerous publications, including the monthly journal *American Psychologist*, the monthly magazine *Monitor on Psychology*, and the quarterly *Journal of Abnormal Psychology*.

Anorexia Nervosa and Bulimia Association (ANAB)
767 Bayridge Dr., PO Box 20058, Kingston, ON K7P 1CO, Canada
e-mail: anab@www.ams.queensu.ca • website: www.phe.queensu.ca/anab/

ANAB is a nonprofit organization made up of health professionals, volunteers, and past and present victims of eating disorders and their families and friends. The association advocates and coordinates support for individuals affected directly or indirectly by eating disorders. As part of its effort to offer a broad range of current information, opinion, and/or advice concerning eating disorders, body image, and related issues, ANAB produces the quarterly newsletter *Reflections*.

Harvard Eating Disorders Center (HEDC)
WACC 725, 15 Parkman St., Boston, MA 02114
(617) 236-7766
e-mail: info@hedc.org • website: www.hedc.org

HEDC works to expand knowledge about eating disorders and their detection, treatment, and prevention through research, education, and outreach. The center lobbies for health policy initiatives on behalf of individuals with eating disorders and promotes the healthy development of women, children, and everyone at risk. HEDC's model education program for adolescent and pre-adolescent girls emphasizes healthy body images, girls' personal power, and overall mental and physical well-being. The center conducts forums and symposia and publishes an annual newsletter.

National Association of Anorexia Nervosa and Associated Disorders (ANAD)
PO Box 7, Highland Park, IL 60035
(847) 831-3438 • fax: (847) 433-4632
website: www.altrue.net/site/anadweb/

ANAD offers hot-line counseling, operates an international network of support groups for people with eating disorders and their families, and provides referrals to health care professionals who treat eating disorders. It produces a quarterly newsletter and information packets and organizes national conferences and local programs. All ANAD services are provided free of charge.

National Eating Disorder Information Centre (NEDIC)
CW 1-211, 200 Elizabeth St., Toronto, ON M5G 2C4, Canada
(866) 633-4220 • (416) 340-4156 • fax: (416) 340-4736
e-mail: nedic@uhn.on.ca • website: www.nedic.ca

NEDIC provides information and resources on eating disorders and weight preoccupation, and it focuses on the sociocultural factors that influence female health-related behaviors NEDIC promotes healthy lifestyles and encourages individuals to make informed choices based on accurate information. It publishes a newsletter and a guide for families and friends of eating-disorder sufferers and sponsors Eating Disorders Awareness Week in Canada

National Eating Disorders Association (NEDA)
603 Stewart St., Suite 803, Seattle, WA 98101
(206) 382-3587
e-mail: info@NationalEatingDisorders.org
website: www.nationaleatingdisorders.org

The largest eating disorders prevention and advocacy group in the world, NEDA represents the merger of Eating Disorders Awareness and Prevention (EDAP), the American Anorexia Bulimia Association (AABA), the National Eating Disorders Organization (NEDO), and Anorexia Nervosa and Related Eating Disorders (ANRED). The association sponsors the annual National Eating Disorders Awareness Week and offers educational outreach programs and training for schools and universities. NEDA publishes a prevention curriculum for grades four through six as well as public prevention and awareness information packets, videos, guides, and other materials.

Society for Adolescent Medicine (SAM)
1916 Copper Oaks Circle, Blue Springs, MO 64015
(816) 224-8010 • fax: (816) 224-8009
e-mail: sam@adolescenthealth.org • website: www.adolescenthealth.org

SAM is a multidisciplinary organization of professionals committed to improving the physical and psychosocial health and well-being of all adolescents. It helps plan and coordinate national and international professional education programs on adolescent health. Its publications include the position paper "Eating Disorders in Adolescents," the monthly *Journal of Adolescent Health*, and the quarterly *SAM Newsletter*.

BIBLIOGRAPHY

Books

Suzanne Abraham and Derek Llewellyn-Jones — *Eating Disorders: The Facts*. New York: Oxford University Press, 2001.

Arnold Andersen, Leigh Cohn, and Thomas Holbrook — *Making Weight: Men's Conflicts with Food, Weight, Shape, and Appearance*. Carlsbad, CA: Gürze Books, 2000.

Frances M. Berg — *Children and Teens Afraid to Eat: Helping Youth in Today's Weight-Obsessed World*. Hettinger, ND: Healthy Weight Network, 2001.

Marlene Boskind-White and William C. White Jr. — *Bulimia/Anorexia: The Binge/Purge Cycle and Self-Starvation*. New York: W.W. Norton, 2000.

Margaret Bullitt-Jonas — *Holy Hunger: A Memoir of Desire*. New York: Knopf, 1999.

Dana K. Cassell — *Food for Thought: The Sourcebook for Obesity and Eating Disorders*. New York: Checkmark Books, 2001.

Peggy Claude-Pierre — *The Secret Language of Eating Disorders: How You Can Understand and Work to Cure Anorexia and Bulimia*. New York: Vintage Books, 1999.

Christopher G. Fairburn and Kelly D. Brownell, eds. — *Eating Disorders and Obesity: A Comprehensive Handbook*. New York: Guilford Press, 2002.

Kathlyn Gay — *Eating Disorders: Anorexia, Bulimia, and Binge Eating*. Berkeley Heights, NJ: Enslow, 2003.

Richard A. Gordon — *Eating Disorders: Anatomy of a Social Epidemic*. Malden, MA: Blackwell, 2000.

Jim Kirkpatrick and Paul Caldwell — *Eating Disorders: Anorexia Nervosa, Bulimia, Binge Eating, and Others*. Buffalo, NY: Firefly Books, 2001.

Michelle Mary Lelwica — *Starving for Salvation: The Spiritual Dimensions of Eating Problems Among American Girls and Women*. New York: Oxford University Press, 1999.

Raymond Lemberg, ed. — *Eating Disorders: A Reference Sourcebook*. Phoenix, AZ: Oryx Press, 1999.

Dawn D. Matthews, ed. — *Eating Disorders Sourcebook: Basic Consumer Health Information About Eating Disorders*. Detroit: Omnigraphics, 2001.

Deborah Marcontell Michel and Susan G. Willard — *When Dieting Becomes Dangerous: A Guide to Understanding and Treating Anorexia and Bulimia*. New Haven, CT: Yale University Press, 2002.

Abigail Natenshon — *When Your Child Has an Eating Disorder: A Step-by-Step Workbook for Parents and Other Caregivers*. San Francisco: Jossey-Bass, 1999.

Carol Emery Normandi and Laurelee Roark — *Over It: A Teen's Guide to Getting Beyond Obsessions with Food and Weight.* Novato, CA: New World Library, 2001.

Carol L. Otis and Roger Goldingay — *The Athletic Woman's Survival Guide: How to Win the Battle Against Eating Disorders, Amenorrhea, and Osteoporosis.* Champaign, IL: Human Kinetics, 2000.

Crystal Phillips — *The Me I Knew I Could Be: One Woman's Journey from 292 Pounds to Peace, Happiness, and Healthy Living.* New York: St. Martin's Press, 2001.

Melissa Spearing — *Eating Disorders: Facts About Eating Disorders and the Search for Solutions.* Bethesda, MD: National Institute of Mental Health, 2001.

Periodicals

Janet Bailey — "Eating Disorders: Are You at Risk?" *Redbook*, October 2002.

Alison Bell — "Disordered Eating: Are You One of the Silent Majority?" *Teen*, February 1999.

Cylin Busby — "Beautiful Girls, Ugly Disease," *Teen*, May 2001.

Nancy Clark — "Starve Wars," *American Fitness*, March 2001.

Kristin Cobb — "His-and-Her Hunger Pangs," *Science News*, July 6, 2002.

Barbara Curtis — "When Dieting Spells Danger," *Christian Parenting Today*, Summer 2002.

Amy Dickinson — "Measuring Up," *Time*, November 20, 2000.

Sharon Epel — "Mom, Am I Fat?" *Ladies Home Journal*, January 2001.

Galina Espinoza — "Diary of a Food Fight," *People*, March 31, 2003.

Beth Gooch — "Losing Friends, Losing Weight, Losing Control," *New York Times Upfront*, April 30, 2001.

Kathy Kaehler — "I Fought Bulimia and Won," *Self*, November 2001.

Claudia Kalb — "When Weight Loss Goes Awry," *Newsweek*, July 3, 2000.

Kathiann M. Kowalski — "Body Image: How Do You See Yourself?" *Current Health 2*, March 2003.

Dawn Mackeen — "Waifs on the Web," *Teen People*, April 1, 2002.

Susan McClelland — "The Lure of the Body Image," *Maclean's*, February 22, 1999.

Richard Morgan — "The Men in the Mirror," *Chronicle of Higher Education*, September 27, 2002.

Alison Motluk — "Born Under a Thin Star," *New Scientist*, August 11, 2001.

P. Myatt Murphy — "Are You Obsessed with Your Body?" *Men's Fitness*, April 2001.

Judith Newman   "Reading, Writing, and Body Appreciation," *Self*, September 2001.

Jennifer Pirtle   "Why Don't They Just Eat?" *Health*, March 2002.

Psychology Today   "Eating Disorders: Girls, Boys, and Bodies," July/August 1999.

Keli Roberts and   "How I Beat Bulimia," *Fitness*, August 2001.
Sally Wadyka

Courtney Rubin   "Losing It," *Washingtonian*, May 2000.

Rebecca Segall   "Never Too Skinny," *Psychology Today*, March/April 2001.

Ellen M. Shaw   "The Dangers of Eating Disorders," *American Fitness*, January/February 2002.

Jenefer Shute and   "Dieting to Death," *Rosie*, November 2001.
Sarah Saffian

Michelle Stacey   "Diary of a Bad Body Image," *Shape*, July 2000.

Mim Udovitch   "A Secret Society of the Starving," *New York Times Magazine*, September 8, 2002.

INDEX